Puzzle Masterpieces

*Elegant Challenges for
Crossword Lovers*

Patrick Berry

**PUZZLE
WRIGHT
PRESS**

An imprint of Sterling
Publishing Co., Inc.
www.puzzlewright.com

Puzzlewright Press and the distinctive Puzzlewright Press logo are trademarks of
Sterling Publishing Co., Inc.

2 4 6 8 10 9 7 5 3 1

Published by Sterling Publishing Co., Inc.
387 Park Avenue South, New York, NY 10016
© 2009 by Patrick Berry
Distributed in Canada by Sterling Publishing
c/o Canadian Manda Group, 165 Dufferin Street
Toronto, Ontario, Canada M6K 3H6
Distributed in the United Kingdom by GMC Distribution Services
Castle Place, 166 High Street, Lewes, East Sussex, England BN7 1XU
Distributed in Australia by Capricorn Link (Australia) Pty. Ltd.
P.O. Box 704, Windsor, NSW 2756, Australia

Printed in China

Sterling ISBN 978-1-4027-6065-5

For information about custom editions, special sales, premium and
corporate purchases, please contact Sterling Special Sales
Department at 800-805-5489 or specialsales@sterlingpublishing.com.

❧ Contents ❧

∽ *Introduction* ∽

As you flip through the pages of this book, you'll see a lot of bizarrely shaped puzzle grids: Figure eights, O-rings, S shapes. Some grids have been designed to resemble objects: a sun, an archery target, a flower garden, a stained glass window. Even the ones that retain the classic square shape of the crossword contain elements you don't usually see in such grids—shaded squares, numbers scattered willy-nilly, and/or an alarming lack of black squares.

I created most of these puzzle forms very early in my constructing career—before I started making crosswords, oddly enough. Initially I was just trying to be different, but I soon learned that variety grids have merits beyond mere difference. For one thing, they tend to contain longer entries, on average, than crossword puzzles. (Entry length is the crossword puzzle's Achilles heel: It's estimated that about 75% of crossword grid entries are five letters or fewer, which makes for a lot of undesirable repetition. By contrast, there are several grid types in this book that don't contain any words of five letters or fewer.)

Then, too, variety puzzles present their own unique challenges to the solver. In some of this book's puzzles, you won't know the lengths of the answers you're looking for. Or you might know what the answer to a given clue is, but you won't know exactly how to enter it in the grid. Or you might be called upon to make deductions—to figure out where an answer probably goes, and then test to see if you're right or wrong. And in some cases you'll enjoy the sublime pleasure of hunting up hidden payoffs (always hinted at in the instructions) after the grid is filled.

That said, I should point out that these puzzles are no more difficult than middle-of-the-week crosswords. Don't let the odd shapes and instructions intimidate you: If you can solve crosswords, you can solve these! I hope you enjoy them.

—Patrick Berry

∽ *Sundial* ∽

This sun-shaped grid will contain 20 seven-letter words and phrases when filled in. Each answer begins in the space next to its corresponding number, continues outward, makes a hairpin turn and ends in the starting space of the following answer.

1 Drink brand whose mascot is known for busting through walls: Hyph.
2 Line drawing in a set of assembly instructions
3 Cosmetics company whose bigwigs drive pink Cadillacs: 2 wds.
4 Region next to Siberia on a Risk board
5 D.C. thoroughfare that's home to lobbyists and think tanks: 2 wds.
6 Reservation for a foursome: 2 wds.
7 Dubai, for one
8 Set of shelves mounted on a toilet tank
9 Satiric utopia created by Samuel Butler
10 Horse with zero chance of winning: Hyph.
11 Criticism
12 Robber who preys on pedestrians
13 Like pinto horses
14 "Hey There ___" (#1 hit for the Plain White T's)
15 Flatfish whose name literally means "flat fish"
16 What a Bundt cake is cooked in: 2 wds.
17 Messy eaters' needs
18 Whines contemptibly
19 Willowy
20 Women's magazine first published in 1903

Solution, page 86

☙ *Some Assembly Required 1* ❧

This 14×14 grid of letters has been chopped into puzzle pieces, and it's up to you to reassemble it. The answer to each numbered clue should be placed in the correspondingly numbered piece, one letter per square, starting in the numbered square. Each row (A–N) in the "tray" contains two answers placed side by side; their clues are given in order, but it's up to you to determine the dividing point between answers. Use the Row answers and the pieces' shapes to determine the proper location of each piece within the tray. You won't need to overlap or rotate any of the pieces. Correctly placed, the 23 pieces will completely fill the tray.

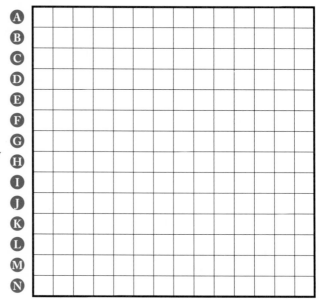

Rows

A Paperwork sent to the IRS
Insulted person's lame comeback: 3 wds.

B Iron ore that's magnetic
Stick in a cage?

C Got away from
And so on and so forth: 2 wds.

D TV show
Eye-opening realization

E Utterly without moisture: 4 wds.
Symbol on Yemen's flag

F Eat like a pig
Good grooming habits

G David's costar on *The X-Files*
Turnkeys at Dartmoor

H They stand in the middles of lanes
Securities that mature in 2 to 10 years: Hyph.

I Wears to check the fit: 2 wds.
What the "P" in P.T. Barnum stands for

J Dallas Mavericks owner Mark
Mike Judge satire about the dumbing down of America

K Fruit with a single large seed
Tosses overboard: Hyph.

L Online buying and selling: Hyph.
Unexpected story development

M Supposed (but not actual) reason
In need of a larger ear trumpet

N Arcade game with ghosts: Hyph.
One drawn in a draft

Pieces

1. TV and newspapers, e.g.: 2 wds.
2. Prepared for Judgment Day
3. IcyHot competitor
4. Wasn't imaginary
5. Adorned with red stones
6. Tile used in a mosaic
7. Sagacious
8. Ancient Greek goddess of agriculture
9. Unidentified
10. How FedEx ships packages
11. Narrator of Ken Burns's *The West*: 2 wds.
12. Prays for the best in the worst circumstances: 3 wds.
13. Universal remedy: Hyph.
14. Sitting pretty: 3 wds.
15. Takes care of: 2 wds.
16. Like asbestos fibers
17. Slimy algae found in stagnant ponds
18. Corporate president who financed Byrd's Antarctic expeditions: 2 wds.
19. Novel that somehow relates to a previous work: 2 wds.
20. Israeli P.M. unseated by Barak
21. Deliberately stilted, as a performance
22. Put a limit on
23. Hot dog condiment

Solution, page 86

∞ *Projectors* ∞

Each puzzle in this set features a series of clues whose answers must be arranged into the square grid provided, reading across and down. All of the answers are one letter too long to fit, however, so each one must project either its first or its last letter outside the grid. (Each grid has two possible arrangements, depending on whether a given answer reads across or down.) Starting at the upper left, the grid's "projectors" will display the name of a famous film reading either clockwise or counterclockwise, like BEN-HUR in the example at right.

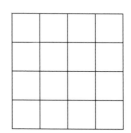

Puzzle 1

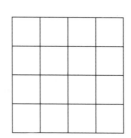

Frida star Hayek
___ male (dominant pack animal)
CD-scanning device
Errors in an e-mail
Story heard at the water cooler
Violent-tempered woman
"Fixes" at the vet's office
Newscaster Zahn

Puzzle 2

Ending for a cabaret club's name: 2 wds.
Country singer Tucker
Hailing from Des Moines
Member of the FBI
Literary device of saying what you don't mean
Winner of four track-and-field golds at the Berlin Games
St. Francis of Assisi, for one
Specialized vocabulary

Puzzle 3

Imitates a lion
Thousand-yard ___ (battle-weary soldier's countenance)
Pleasing scent
Blue-skinned denizen of 1980s TV
Become less intense
Winter afflictions
Stop the flow of, as a river: 2 wds.
Tuesdays With Morrie author Mitch

Puzzle 4

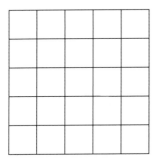

Deerstalker-wearing
   sleuth
Deal or No Deal host
Licentious
Children of a ___ God
Nickname for a five iron
Window that projects from
   a sloping roof
Some *Dancing With the Stars*
   tunes
Heavenly messengers
Sunday supplement, e.g.
Organic compounds found
   in wine

Puzzle 5

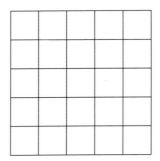

"___ for Captain Spaulding"
   (song from *Animal Crackers*)
Gentle rub
Uninspired use of old
   material
Iraqi currency
One who stocks up food in jars
"Tennis ___?"
Put a value on
Nairobi native
Ecclesiastical rules
No longer edible, as butter

Puzzle 6

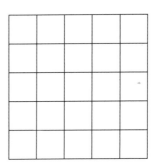

Resign oneself to the truth,
   slangily: 2 wds.
Popular pet parrot
Communicate, as info
Remington ___ (1980s TV
   show)
Fat Man and Little Boy, for
   two: Hyph.
Encircled with a belt
"The door's open!": 2 wds.
Windowframe's top
Muffle
Paddle waver at an auction

❧ *Rows Garden 1* ❧

Words fit into this flower garden in two ways. Row answers read horizontally from the lettered markers; each Row contains two consecutive answers reading left to right (except Rows A and L, which contain one answer reading across the nine protruding spaces). Blooms are six-letter words or phrases that fill the colored hexagons, reading either clockwise or counterclockwise. Bloom clues are divided into three lists, White, Pink, and Gray; answers from each list should be placed only in the appropriately colored hexagons. All three Bloom lists are in random order, so you must use the Row answers to figure out where to plant each Bloom.

Rows

A Flowering plant with large coin-shaped seeds

B "Bullet With Butterfly Wings" band, with "the": 2 wds.
Chapter 11 declarer's burdens

C Singer called "Lefty Wilbury" on the one album he recorded with the Traveling Wilburys: 2 wds.
"As if it makes any difference to me": 4 wds.

D Multivitamin brand name that's also the recommended dosage: 3 wds.
Pictures in which black is white and vice versa: 2 wds.

E Bad blood: 2 wds.
Rings tossed at sea: 2 wds.

F Neil Diamond song made famous by UB40: 3 wds.
Lacking in importance or substance

G *Time* voted him "Person of the Century" in 1999: 2 wds.
Fruit whose name is Cantonese for "gold orange"

H Literary character who was outed in 2007
Hospital doctor's circuit: 2 wds.

I Best Actress nominee for 1993's *Shadowlands*: 2 wds.
Misses a morning class, maybe

J Big-time incentive to accept an early retirement: 2 wds.
Available if needed, as a résumé: 2 wds.

K Scrupulously avoids using: 3 wds.
Surreal 2005 Terry Gilliam film that bombed in theaters

L 1992 Summer Olympics host city

White Blooms

Former Giants manager Alou
Steel rods embedded in concrete
Sitting for a portrait
Billy who directed *Double Indemnity*
Scatters money around
Removed complexity from, with "down"
De Niro's *Midnight Run* costar
Part of FDR
Most empty
City leaders
One who's tuned in
King of songwriting
Stable that rents out horses
Poet Philip or shortstop Barry

Pink Blooms

Creator of No. 5 perfume
Struck with a fist
Type of clef
"Time to run": 2 wds.

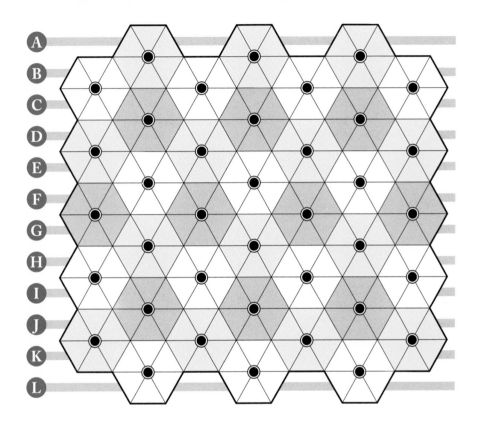

Categories on Netflix's page
Executed perfectly, as a dismount
"The Birthplace of America," to residents
Improvise as you go: 2 wds.
1862 Civil War battle site in Tennessee
"___ Fideles"

Minimum number required to be present
Jazz legend Hampton
Lops off
Large taxonomic subdivision

Gray Blooms
Jug head?
Walking: 2 wds.

Instructed
On another continent
Propped (up)
Chessman capable of jumping other pieces
Made an air horn's sound
Iconic role for Newman
Name in an A.A. Milne title
Like this clue's type

Solution, page 86

13 ∞

❧ Boxing Rings 1 ❧

The answer to each clue below is entered into the grid as a rectangular "ring" of letters, starting in the numbered space and proceeding clockwise. Each answer begins at one corner of its ring; the symbol before each clue indicates which corner of the ring (so, for example, the answer to clue 1 begins in the upper left corner of its ring). If the answer to #1 were RINGSIDE, it would be arranged in one of the rings shown. The numbers in parentheses after the clues indicate the length of the answer words. If you place all the answers correctly, every space in the grid will be used, and the shaded spaces will contain a well-turned phrase.

¹R	I	N
E		G
D	I	S

¹R	I
E	N
D	G
I	S

¹R	I	N	G
E	D	I	S

1 They're handy with retorts (8)

2 Revenue collectors (6)

3 Garter materials (8)

3 Become more intense (8)

4 Sneaky plan (6)

5 Ammo for a gun used in emergencies (6)

6 Rain cloud (6)

7 French port nearest England's coast (6)

8 Belonging to a large combat unit (10)

9 Means of forecasting election results (4,4)

10 Narrower at one end, like an obelisk (8)

11 Dumas described it as "other people's money" (8)

12 Vehicle used in Arctic exploration (3-3)

13 Win over (8)

13 Wines beloved by Miles in *Sideways* (5,5)

14 Insects with bright red wings (8)

15 The world's bestselling battery brand (8)

16 Noisy disturbances (8)

17 American equivalent of a Brit's "Year 2" (5,5)

18 Get a wrong idea about (8)

19 Process of calling the phone number stuck to a credit card (10)

20 One of many sold for a school-band fundraiser (5,3)

21 "That's enough!" (3,3,2)

22 Give lift to (8)

23 Forms of an element with different neutron counts (8)

24 They may help clear the set (6,4)

25 Theatrical agent's fee, often (3,7)

26 Pierce's original bunkie on *M*A*S*H* (8)

27 Injury suitable for a Band-Aid (8)

27 Part of the process of last rites (10)

28 How blue states tend to vote (10)

29 Fuel rod containers (8)

30 Neuroimaging device (3,7)

31 Awareness (10)

32 The Ancient Wonders of the World, e.g. (6)

33 One whose business is looking up? (10)

34 Delicacy made with phyllo (6)

35 Train robber's "disguise" (8)

36 Queue area outside an airport (8)

Snake Charmer 1

Enter the answer to each clue into the grid, starting in the correspondingly numbered space and proceeding clockwise around the S to end in the space before the next consecutive number. The chain of 24 answer words will snake its way around the grid twice.

1 Tennis champ Gibson
2 Sent up the river: 3 wds.
3 From North Africa
4 Mockumentary director Christopher
5 Alcoholic beverage known as "the green fairy"
6 Jim who voiced Mr. Magoo
7 Greek god who wears winged sandals
8 Italian dish of sautéed veal
9 Less pricey than usual: 2 wds.
10 *Gladiator* setting
11 Best Supporting Actress winner for *West Side Story*: 2 wds.
12 NaCl, more familiarly: 2 wds.
13 The U.K.'s biggest airport
14 Black-clad baddie in a martial-arts film
15 Ingrid's *Casablanca* role
16 Speech given from a soapbox
17 Cruelly betrays: 4 wds.
18 Multiplex employee
19 Bugle signal played thrice daily on army bases: 2 wds.
20 Expert witnesses are allowed to offer them
21 Last Oldsmobile to be produced
22 Good reason for a promotion
23 "That's ___" (Dean Martin song)
24 Very important people

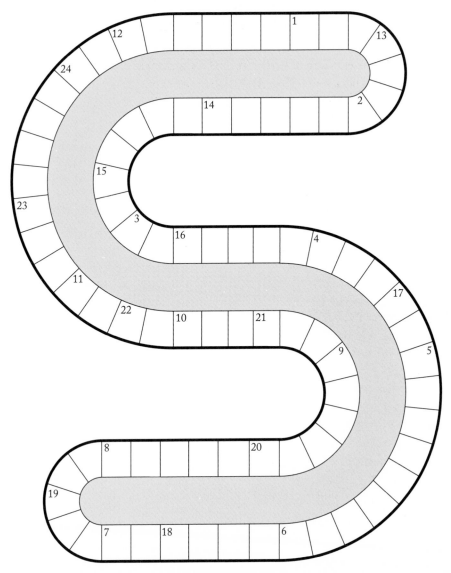

∽ Cloud Nine ∽

Each answer in this puzzle is nine letters long and encircles the correspondingly numbered triangle in the grid, proceeding either clockwise (+) or counterclockwise (−) as indicated at the end of each clue. It's up to you to determine the starting point of each answer. When the grid is filled, you'll find an appropriate musical question in the cloud's "silver linings."

1 Footwear with tiny spikes set into the soles: 2 wds. (−)
2 Removed, as a mustache: 2 wds. (+)
3 Where Cain was banished after murdering Abel: 3 wds. (−)
4 Wilbur Post's portrayer on *Mister Ed*: 2 wds. (+)
5 Horrendous (−)
6 Bugle calls heard at sunrise (−)
7 Seat for Lady Godiva (−)
8 ___ motion (what Kepler's laws pertain to) (+)
9 Author of campaign-button catchphrases (−)
10 Secures a copy from Amazon before the release date (+)
11 Kept going in spite of hardships: 2 wds. (−)
12 Primate such as a gibbon or siamang: 2 wds. (−)
13 Fruit that's juiced to make mai tais (−)

14 Not particularly efficient, as a solution (+)
15 Transatlantic Morse code message (−)
16 Possible reason for an unrestful sleep (−)
17 Freed from an oppressor (+)
18 Like bloodhounds and spaniels: Hyph. (−)
19 "___ on My Guitar" (Taylor Swift song) (+)
20 Portable cooker used by backpackers: 2 wds. (−)
21 One accompanying a reporter for on-location work (+)
22 Spies use them to protect their identities: 2 wds. (+)
23 Creator of Don Quixote and Sancho Panza (−)
24 Show genre typified by *Survivor*: 2 wds. (−)
25 Atomic number of uranium: Hyph. (−)

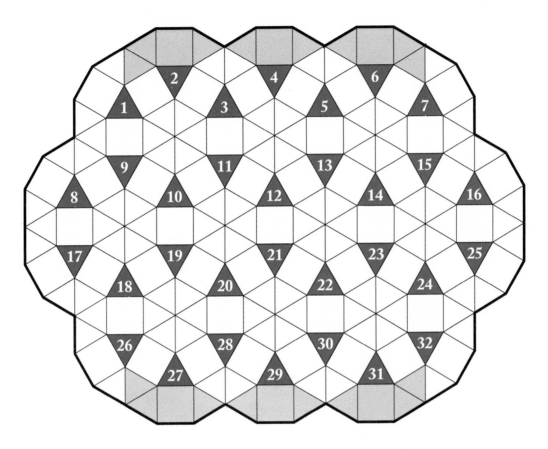

26 Catlike carnivores kept as vermin-killing pets in India (+)

27 What a detective needs to clear up before closing the case: 2 wds (−)

28 Hippie's necklace: 2 wds. (+)

29 Sign of life (−)

30 Began with: 2 wds. (+)

31 Restrict the movement of (−)

32 "___ of the Willing" (Bush-era catchphrase) (+)

Solution, page 87

Game Hunting

Each row and column of this grid contains a series of answers placed end to end; clues are given in order, but the dividing points between answers are for you to determine. When the grid is filled, go hunting for six quarries hidden diagonally in the grid (as in a word search) and circle their letters. Quarries will all be at least five letters long and fit into a certain category. Once you've found all six, the circled letters on the gunsight's shaded spaces (read from left to right and top to bottom) will reveal the true quarries here.

Rows

1 Refuse to cooperate
Loses one's footing
Phoned: 2 wds.

2 ___ acid (protein building block)
"Esto perpetua" is its motto
Ancient longship sailors

3 Kitchen set
More kitschy

4 Better chance of winning
Listen to
Royal messengers

5 Citrus farmer
Airline-seat choice
Muppet who owns a goldfish named Dorothy

6 Office dogsbodies
Brazilian musical genre
Word after more or less

7 Andy Taylor issued Barney Fife only one
Waitress's burden
Finely honed

8 *Live at* ___ (1970 Who album)
Suggestive, as a story
Kiefer's *Young Guns* costar

9 Since: 2 wds.
Graphical user interface features

10 This-night-only entrée
One of Gehrig's 1,995: Abbr.
Positive feature

11 Pal of Frodo
R&B singer ___ K-Doe
Wax lyrical

12 Lacking room to grow in, as teeth
Alias lead-in
Scary Movie actress Faris

13 Match makers?
5th-century invaders
Ask for more of, in a way

14 Lotion ingredient
CPR expert
___ Theatre (WWII combat region)

15 Gridiron measures
Tout de suite
Daisy Dukes, e.g.

Columns

1 Ne'er-do-well: 2 wds.
Rapturous delight
"Goodness gracious!": 2 wds.

2 Surrounded by
French city where Joan of Arc was martyred
Samuel Richardson novel

3 Industry terms
Coat checker's find?
Caveat ___

4 Last word of "Oh! Susanna"
Uses a blowtorch
Came to an end

5 "Put that in your pipe and smoke it!": 2 wds.
Sooty stains

6 Bottled water units
Away from one's desk?
Actress Thurman

7 Genesis of a plan
Four-legged film star of yore
Lawyer's customers

8 Any of Jacob's sons
It encompasses the Gulf of Suez: 2 wds.

9 Iranian monarchs
Apocalypto people
Handle adversity well: 2 wds.

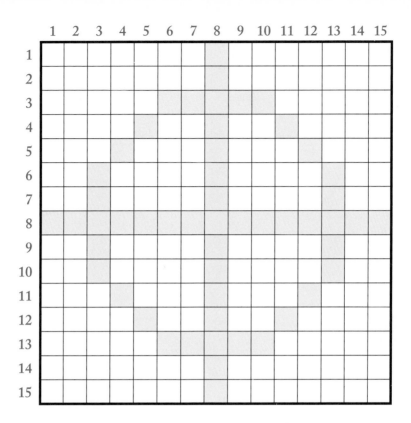

	1	2	3	4	5	6	7	8	9	10	11	12	13	14	15

10 Spiked wheel on a cowboy
    boot
    "Time for me to get a move
    on!"
    Fishing-line weights
11 San ___ fault
    Mazda convertible
    "Doesn't that look nice!"

12 ___ Helmer (*A Doll's House*
    heroine)
    Study of right and wrong
    Marx brother whose real
    name was Arthur
13 Yakitori cooker
    Popular Xbox game series
    Split in two

14 Like secondhand goods
    "Tell it to the ___"
    Not mixed with anything, to
    bartenders
15 First-___ shooter (video
    game type)
    Newsgroup message
    Justifiably receives

Solution, page 87

∽ *Some Assembly Required 2* ∽

This 14×14 grid of letters has been chopped into puzzle pieces, and it's up to you to reassemble it. The answer to each numbered clue should be placed in the correspondingly numbered piece, one letter per square, starting in the numbered square. Each row (A–N) in the "tray" contains two answers placed side by side; their clues are given in order, but it's up to you to determine the dividing point between answers. Use the Row answers and the pieces' shapes to determine the proper location of each piece within the tray. You won't need to overlap or rotate any of the pieces. Correctly placed, the 23 pieces will completely fill the tray.

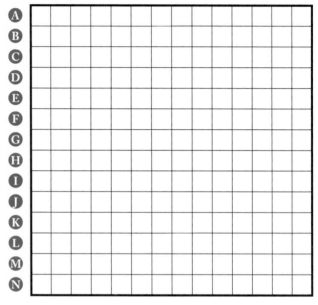

Rows

A Name seen on oil tankers
1950 film that won the Best Song Oscar for "Bibbidi-Bobbidi-Boo"

B 1980s music store wares
Archaeological find

C Crying like a baby
Not at all worldly

D "___ is only a larger kind of going abroad": Samuel Butler
San Francisco transports: 2 wds.

E Spine-tingling
Added insult to injury, slangily: 3 wds.

F Arrest sheet entry
Sunday in New York composer: 2 wds.

G Into small pieces
Let's-all-show-respect command: 2 wds.

H Leather-bound books
Deciding on: 2 wds.

I Utmost extent: 2 wds.
Scavenging birds seen on shorelines

J Suited to the occasion
Oft-rented outfits

K Frequent *Ugly Betty* guest star Hayek
Shirley Temple ingredient: 2 wds.

L Resistances to certain diseases
Richness, to a winetaster

M Dish made from brisket: 2 wds.
Baby carrier parts

N Opponent who will never bury the hatchet: 2 wds.
Takes to court

Pieces

1 Twinkling effect
2 Like Reach toothbrushes
3 Tight-___ (taciturn)
4 Desktop devices first sold in 1958
5 Price war participants
6 Join, as a meeting: 3 wds.
7 Some straight-ticket voters: 2 wds.
8 BlackBerrys, e.g.
9 Whisky chaser?: 3 wds.
10 Unsupported, in a way
11 Body of water shared by Honduras, Nicaragua, and El Salvador: 3 wds.
12 Gift for a brainy kid: 2 wds.
13 Garage band's recording: 2 wds.
14 One who speaks for others
15 Direction toward which the Earth rotates
16 Platitude from a listener who isn't really listening: 2 wds.
17 Deceased TV pitchman digitally brought back to life in a 2007 ad: 2 wds.
18 Marsh grasses
19 Person born on Valentine's Day, e.g.
20 Wanderer detained by Calypso
21 They're not people persons
22 Host of the 1950s show *See It Now*
23 Smoothly switching topics

Solution, page 88

~ *Snake Charmer 2* ~

Enter the answer to each clue into the grid, starting in the correspondingly numbered space and proceeding clockwise around the S to end in the space before the next consecutive number. The chain of 25 answer words will snake its way around the grid twice.

1 Ignominious scoreboard position
2 Appliance needed to prepare mint juleps: 2 wds.
3 *The Tailor of* ___ (John le Carré novel)
4 Steel-cage arena in a Mad Max film
5 Long speech full of invective
6 26th of July Movement founder
7 Chocolate syrup famously used as fake blood in Hitchcock's *Psycho*
8 De Niro's *Raging Bull* costar
9 Vacation home in Tuscany
10 Obligatory line in a knock-knock joke: 2 wds.
11 With desperate energy: 3 wds.
12 Charmingly spritely
13 Material found in fitted sheets
14 Pale brown shade
15 Porter on a Himalayan expedition
16 Jets quarterback voted MVP of Super Bowl III
17 Remove from the oven too soon
18 Word following mass or mixed
19 Manhattan neighborhood that stages an annual film festival
20 Flashing disco lamps
21 Body of regulations that affect average Joes: 2 wds.
22 Multitude
23 Cattle breed from England
24 Thomas Cromwell's title
25 Beatles #1 hit that begins "Baby's good to me": 3 wds.

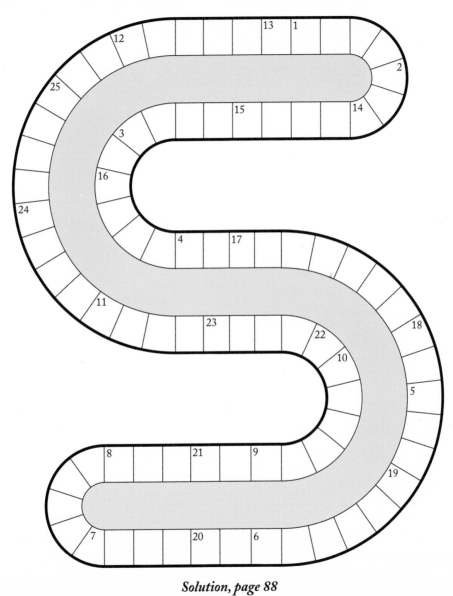

Solution, page 88

∞ *Riding the Waves* ∞

In this puzzle Row answers read straight across the grid's rows, while Wave answers follow the zigzag paths indicated by the grid's shading. Each Row and Wave contains a series of answers placed end to end; answers are clued in order, but the dividing points between them are for you to determine. The letters in the protruding spaces at the top and bottom of the grid will spell an appropriate resting place when you're done riding the waves.

Rows

1 School that's home to the Whiffenpoofs
No-no in objective news stories
Instances of good behavior

2 Be in cahoots (with)
Without a female companion
2001 thriller starring Tilda Swinton: 3 wds.

3 Survive, but only just: 2 wds.
Fortified dessert wine
Burrowing mammal whose name literally means "earth pig"

4 Almost frightening enthusiasm
Language also known as "modern Persian"
Likely candidates for the cover of *SI*'s Swimsuit Issue

5 Read intently: 2 wds.
On neither side
Afternoon snooze

6 Unimpressive display of manners: 2 wds.
Director and star of 1992's *Of Mice and Men*
Kitschy 1960s "big hair" styles

7 Crashers at a concert?
Gets the better of
Make an allusion (to)

8 Engine component that increases speed
Portrayer of TV's Norm Peterson: 2 wds.
Mineral that's 8 on the Mohs hardness scale

9 Member of the world's third-largest religion
Shaggy-dog story
Sandwich board wearer's hangout: 2 wds.

Waves

2 Found by chance: 2 wds.
Sense that doesn't require the use of the head
Okay in theory but perhaps not in practice

3 Exclamation from Jimmy Olsen
Item inserted into a DVD player
Like all reindeer
Baby boy : blue :: baby girl : ___

4 Australian opera singer Nellie
Tablet kept beside a phone: 2 wds.
Robots designed to explore the surface of a planet

5 Set out?: 2 wds.
Queen ___ (*Star Wars Episode I: The Phantom Menace* character)

6 Fido's prize
Reproductive glands
Large proof-of-purchase slips: 2 wds.

7 Passengers' fees
Fit only for throwing away
Vertical face of a stair

1

2

3

4

5

6

7

8

9

10

8 ___ Man (bizarre 1970s advertising
   mascot who captained a tiny
   boat): Hyph.
   Abby and Martha's nephew in *Arsenic
   and Old Lace*
   Dreyfuss's costar in the 1987 action-comedy
   Stakeout

9 The Scarecrow accuses the Wizard of being
   one in *The Wizard of Oz*
   ___ *in the Key of Life* (Stevie Wonder album)
   Got a bit carried away: 3 wds.

10 Hang on the line?: Hyph.
   Item on a chalkrail
   Honored guests walk on it: 2 wds.

Solution, page 88

Rows Garden 2

Words fit into this flower garden in two ways. Row answers read horizontally from the lettered markers; each Row contains two consecutive answers reading left to right (except Rows A and L, which contain one answer reading across the nine protruding spaces). Blooms are six-letter words or phrases that fill the colored hexagons, reading either clockwise or counterclockwise. Bloom clues are divided into three lists, White, Pink, and Gray; answers from each list should be placed only in the appropriately colored hexagons. All three Bloom lists are in random order, so you must use the Row answers to figure out where to plant each Bloom.

Rows

A Flowering plant whose fruits burst open if touched

B First American artist to cover a Beatles song ("From Me to You"): 2 wds.
Carnival barker's refrain: 3 wds.

C Easily set off, as one's temper: Hyph.
Hummingbird feeder's contents: 2 wds.

D Lead-in for an ironic reminder: 3 wds.
Little something before the entrée

E Sweet Valentine's Day delivery?
Treat that's alternately licked and crunched: 2 wds., hyph.

F Author of the 1952 baseball novel *The Natural*: 2 wds.
In theory but not in practice: 2 wds.

G Classic card game that mimics a road race: 2 wds.
Thing that can change your perception?: 2 wds.

H Desperate pass?: 2 wds.
Extreme's only Billboard #1 hit: 3 wds.

I Actor who played the Joker on TV's *Batman*: 2 wds.
Met one's match?: 3 wds.

J Tangy jam that contains fruit peel: 2 wds.
Made the most of a dramatic scene

K Donovan song that begins with the lyric "I'm just mad about saffron": 2 wds.
Hip-hop hit by Young MC: 3 wds.

L Looney Tunes character who's known for shouting "Sufferin' succotash!"

White Blooms

Word afore aforethought
What golfers call the "short club"
Head, slangily
One-horse carriage
Predators who hunt in packs
Not merely harmful to your health
Fred of *The Love Boat* who later became a congressman
Make a difference
Dot-eater of arcade fame: Hyph.
How bumper-to-bumper traffic moves
Birthplace of Franz Kafka
Rained icy pellets
Signature song of *Cats*
Large numbers

Pink Blooms

Ingratiating to an annoying degree
Disposition of the troops
Make some changes in the urban planning

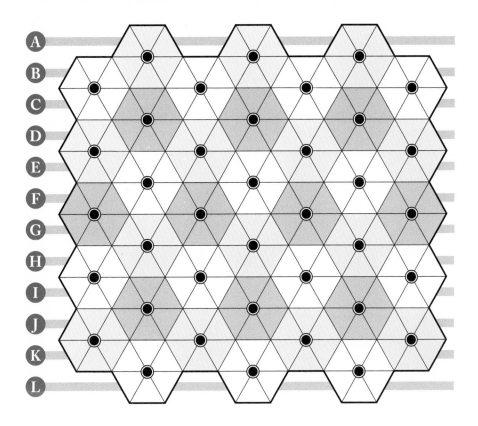

NFL team formerly known as
    the Oilers
Exploited, as a privilege
Swiss district
Possessing
Scrooge's late business partner
Unfortunate occurrence
TV show that used the pitch
    line "Save the cheerleader,
    save the world"

Telephone company nickname
    before a 1984 breakup: 2 wds.
Horses' cries
Dedicate, as a song
Icing on the cake

Gray Blooms
Flexible
Requiring fancy dress
One is worn at age one

Snappy comeback
State policeman in Texas
E-mail software named after a
    famous writer
Certain baseball cards
It means "stirred noodles" in
    Chinese: 2 wds.
Two-time NBA All-Star
    Dennis
Special announcer?

Solution, page 88

Block Lettering

The answers in this puzzle are all five-letter words with no repeated letters. Each answer should be placed in the correspondingly numbered block, with the first letter (the initial) in the shaded square and the remaining letters (the filler) in the white space, as in the example shown. Solving one block will help you figure out others; the initial of a given block will appear in the fillers of all horizontally and vertically adjacent blocks. (This rule has many implications! Use deductive reasoning.)

M | ODEL

1 Patriots' Day month
2 Lumber jacket pattern
3 *El Cantante* star Jennifer
4 Woody Allen's last movie, alphabetically speaking
5 Flower girl from *Pygmalion*
6 Pterodactyl-like monster of classic cinema
7 Lozenges
8 Eyed impertinently
9 Doohickey
10 Public perception
11 Mythology featuring Valkyries
12 Car that seats four comfortably
13 Where the second leg of the English Triple Crown is run
14 Blue-haired TV matriarch
15 Self-evident truth

16 Where the earth's crust is at its thinnest
17 "The Tortoise and the Hare" author
18 Hester Prynne's illegitimate daughter
19 Frolics
20 Daytime talk show, for short
21 Ancient manuscript
22 Show of brilliance
23 Fall into old, bad habits
24 Drink tea noisily
25 Holier-than-thou
26 Brand of knife sold at craft stores: Hyph.
27 LBJ's home state
28 Josh Baskin becomes one in *Big*
29 Carrier name phased out in 1996
30 Two cents
31 Drive train parts

1	2	3	4	5
6	7	8	9	10
11	12	13	14	15
16	17	18	19	20
21	22	23	24	25
26	27	28	29	30
31	32	33	34	35
36	37	38	39	40

32 Witness's place in a courtroom
33 Makes a sketch
34 Like poker chips
35 More upscale, as a neighborhood
36 Dasani competitor

37 19th-century child laborer seen on street corners
38 Souvenir from a war
39 Ball team bigwig
40 Dark ornamental wood

Solution, page 89

∽ *Twist Ties* ∽

The answers in this puzzle are all seven-letter words or phrases in which the second and sixth letters are the same. Each answer twists around its corresponding number in the grid, starting in one of the innermost diamond-shaped spaces and ending in the adjacent space. As shown in the example HORIZON, there are two possible placements for each answer; it's up to you to determine which is correct.

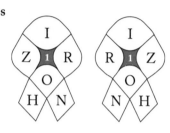

1 Sea creature with radial symmetry
2 Logos
3 Mosquito fleet's makeup: 2 wds.
4 Candidate's first hurdle
5 Act in accordance with: 2 wds.
6 Brand of powdered coffee additive
7 Suddenly stops running, as an engine: 2 wds.
8 Vain young go-getter
9 Wisconsin city on Lake Winnebago
10 Skill on the stump
11 Without a doubt
12 Preferred type of flight
13 Turn the tables: 2 wds.
14 Committing one of the seven deadly sins
15 "The sweet ___" (boxing)
16 Bus stop fixtures
17 Integrated circuit that contains organics
18 Explosive energy of a missile
19 Not here yet, say
20 Counting everyone: 2 wds.

Solution, page 89

Snake Charmer 3

Enter the answer to each clue into the grid, starting in the correspondingly numbered space and proceeding clockwise around the S to end in the space before the next consecutive number. The chain of 24 answer words will snake its way around the grid twice.

1 Napoleon Dynamite exclamation
2 Without a scratch
3 ___ Purina Company (firm bought out by Nestlé in 2002)
4 Herb believed to minimize cold symptoms
5 Avails oneself of
6 Rum-and-cola cocktail: 2 wds.
7 Goddess who turned Arachne into a spider
8 Most prestigious prize at Cannes: 2 wds.
9 Purple-clad superhero of comic strips, with "the"
10 Pigtail
11 Shakespeare's *The Comedy of* ___
12 Dances with a quick three-step movement: Hyph.
13 Bravely endure
14 Stays away from
15 Coventry landmark
16 Dense pottery: 2 wds.
17 Last Communist leader of Romania
18 Indonesian island that hosted the 2007 U.N. Climate Change Conference
19 Be exposed to air, as wine
20 Attacked with firebombs
21 Harry Potter, for one
22 Video game series featuring Lara Croft: 2 wds.
23 Psychiatrist who invented the inkblot test
24 How something might be torn

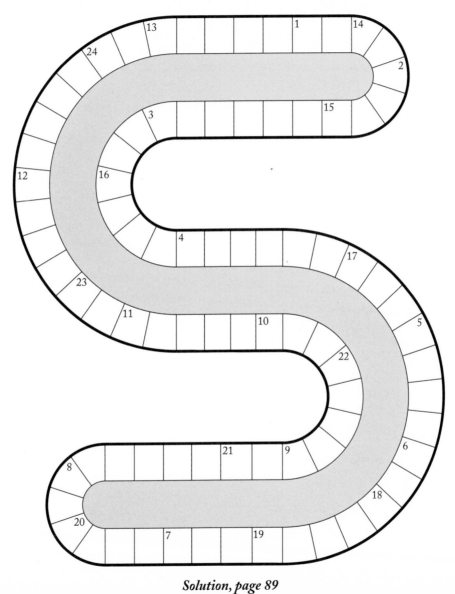

Solution, page 89

Boxing Rings 2

The answer to each clue below is entered into the grid as a rectangular "ring" of letters, starting in the numbered space and proceeding clockwise. Each answer begins at one corner of its ring; the symbol before each clue indicates which corner of the ring (so, for example, the answer to clue 1 begins in the upper left corner of its ring). If the answer to #1 were RINGSIDE, it would be arranged in one of the rings shown. The numbers in parentheses after the clues indicate the length of the answer words. If you place all the answers correctly, every space in the grid will be used, and the shaded spaces will contain a well-turned phrase.

¹R	I	N
E		G
D	I	S

¹R	I
E	N
D	G
I	S

¹R	I	N	G
E	D	I	S

1 "Soak Up the Sun" singer (6,4)
2 How robots might be operated (8)
3 Fictional astronaut in David Bowie's "Space Oddity" (5,3)
4 Broken in two (8)
5 Blind alleys (4,4)
6 Adherence to the formalities (8)
7 Oscar-winning role for Hopkins (6)
8 "The Listeners" poet Walter (2,2,4)
9 Logged into (8)
10 Grim time for investors (4,6)
11 Part of a British prep-school outfit (4,6)
12 Religious group that refuses to bear arms or take oaths (10)
13 What swords are beaten into during peacetime (10)
14 Restaurants that offer scones and crumpets (8)
15 More unctuous (8)
16 Post-op souvenirs (8)
17 Goes where no one's gone before (8)
18 Three Tenors member (8)
19 Less assertive (6)
19 One-man underwater vessels (8)

20 On the sly (2,6)
21 One-sixth of a year (8)
22 Facetious title for a mayor (8)
23 Discus champ who carried the torch into the stadium at the 1996 Games (2,6)
24 100-to-0 loss, slangily (8)
25 Bodysuits (8)
26 Making good as new (10)
27 Dante Alighieri's birthplace (8)
28 Devotees of Austen (8)
29 Screenwriter Larry Cohen's follow-up to *Phone Booth* (8)
30 First-inning pitchers (8)
31 Argentina fits entirely into one (4,4)
32 Put forward (8)
33 Valley created by running water (6)
34 Cheese used in cheese sticks (10)
35 Like Scrooge's Christmas-eve visitors (8)
35 Casablanca and Cartagena, for two (8)
36 TV personality idolized by *SCTV* character Ed Grimley (3,5)
37 Indifferent to right and wrong (6)
38 Small round headpiece (8)

Packing Slips

Answers fit into this grid in two ways. Each Row contains a series of answers placed end to end, clued in order of appearance. Answers to clues in the Crates list must be packed into rectangular containers before entering. Letters in a given Crate should be packed left-to-right and top-to-bottom, as shown in the SAMPLE at right. Crate clues are ordered by length (shown in parentheses after each clue) but otherwise randomly, so you must use the Row answers to determine where each Crate belongs. The 22 Crates will *almost* fill the grid; the remaining unpacked letters, read from left to right by rows, will spell an appropriate phrase.

S	A	M
P	L	E

S	A
M	P
L	E

Rows

1 From that time on
   Florida city where the Dodgers do their spring training: 2 wds.

2 Catch up with: 2 wds.
   Separate into piles
   At rest

3 Largest of the Balkan States
   Most prone to boasting, perhaps

4 Fruit-flavored soda sold by the Coca-Cola Company
   Greenhouse containers
   Inscription on a coat of arms

5 Consistently poor performer
   People who do as they're told
   Birds seen on Canadian dollar coins

6 Point fingers at
   The book of Deuteronomy contains his final teachings
   Barely detectable

7 Round number?
   Plum pudding tidbit
   "Pearls Before ___"

8 Cigar that's nearly finished
   "It's time for dinner!": 2 wds.
   Likely Christmas-shopping stop

9 German chancellor Merkel
   Document that proves ownership: 2 wds.

10 Trouser material
   Groom's attendant
   Vowel sound common to unstressed syllables

11 Old Testament book that precedes Job
   "What a cool trick!"
   Necessity in making refried beans

12 Clog up
   Row of seats in an amphitheater
   1970s Yankees pitcher Sparky

13 *Flushed Away* animals
   Taken in
   Rod embedded in concrete

14 Coming through the entrance
   Tupperware pieces
   Unit of volume used for firewood

15 *Das Kapital* author
   Manchester United player Rooney
   Fish-eating mammals

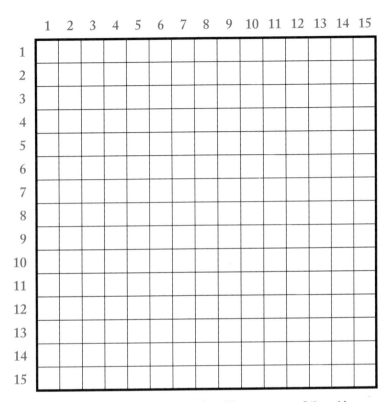

	1	2	3	4	5	6	7	8	9	10	11	12	13	14	15
1															
2															
3															
4															
5															
6															
7															
8															
9															
10															
11															
12															
13															
14															
15															

Crates

Film director Bergman (6)

Slender candles (6)

On this date (6)

"I grant all of that, but…" (4,2)

Sealed envelope given to a commander (6)

Sports jacket (6)

Graphic in a history text (8)

"Good for you!" (8)

Thurman's costar in *The Truth About Cats & Dogs* (8)

Stops, as blood flow (8)

Slave whose suit for freedom was brought before the Supreme Court (4,5)

Red-letter (9)

Film that netted Pauly Shore a Razzie for Worst New Star (6,3)

Full of research and big words (9)

Ideal example (10)

Poet who coined the nonsense term "runcible spoon" (6,4)

Like cold consommés (10)

Prisoner known as the Birdman of Alcatraz (6,6)

Blithe comment after a loss (4,3,2,3)

The Short Happy Life of Francis Macomber author (6,9)

They join your calf muscles to your heel bones (8,7)

1993 romantic comedy that frequently references *An Affair to Remember* (9,2,7)

Solution, page 90

∽ *Rows Garden 3* ∽

Words fit into this flower garden in two ways. Row answers read horizontally from the lettered markers; each Row contains two consecutive answers reading left to right (except Rows A and L, which contain one answer reading across the nine protruding spaces). Blooms are six-letter words or phrases that fill the colored hexagons, reading either clockwise or counterclockwise. Bloom clues are divided into three lists, White, Pink, and Gray; answers from each list should be placed only in the appropriately colored hexagons. All three Bloom lists are in random order, so you must use the Row answers to figure out where to plant each Bloom.

Rows

A *The Purple Rose of Cairo* star: 2 wds.

B Unlikely to appreciate blue humor: Hyph.
Way to order fried eggs: 2 wds.

C Gleaming kitchen countertop material: 2 wds.
It's also known as "store cheese"

D Russian-sounding entrée invented by a French chef: 2 wds.
Subtly points someone in the right direction: 3 wds.

E What strong backlighting reduces an object to
NFL Commissioner for the first 23 Super Bowls: 2 wds.

F Marine arthropod with a heavy round exoskeleton: 2 wds.
Bright means of attracting customers?: 2 wds.

G Lawyer who defended Leopold and Loeb: 2 wds.
Morning show?

H First African-American White House television correspondent: 2 wds.
Wilkie Collins novel about a stolen Indian diamond: 2 wds.

I Saved money on gas, perhaps
Accident that barely even seems worth reporting: 2 wds.

J Choice seating area in a theater or opera house: 2 wds.
Females who have kids?: 2 wds.

K As quick as a wink: 5 wds.
Emperor whose reign ushered in the Pax Romana

L De rigueur

White Blooms

Secured to a dock
Four are required before building a hotel in Monopoly
Chemical element discovered by the Curies
Become aware of
Gets going
Guy from *Memento*
Altered by decorators
Astrological symbol preceding the scorpion
Spoke for all to hear
Alarm clock button
Schedules
Good at solving problems
Like cotton candy
Made steady

Pink Blooms

Gilda in the original *SNL* troupe
Top of a doorframe
Moved stealthily, as one's hand
What many dates center around

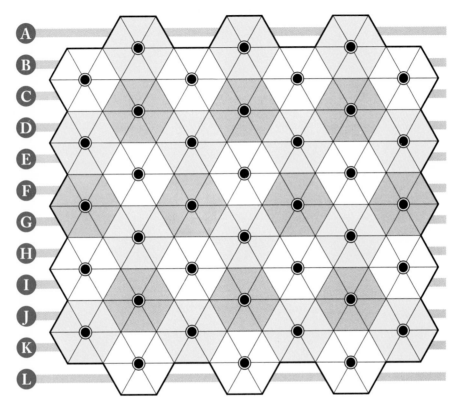

Litter member
Social position
Ukrainian peninsula
Hat worn by Indiana Jones
"I Get a Kick out of You"
    composer
Remember the ___ (2000 Denzel
    Washington film)
Reddish rum cocktail: 2 wds.
Somewhat

Bar and grill chain with an
    "Awesome Blossom"
    on its appetizer menu
Like the Oscars ceremony

Gray Blooms
___ interests
Seed used to make five-spice
    powder
Resounded

The Little ___ *That Could*
    (famous children's book)
Servers at Baskin-Robbins?
Chopped into small pieces
Metal found in all U.S. coins
    except the penny
Like days of yore
Many English soldiers at
    Agincourt
Like glee club music

Solution, page 90

Seven Sages

Each answer in this puzzle is seven letters long and encircles the correspondingly numbered space, reading either clockwise (+) or counterclockwise (−) as indicated. The starting point of each answer is for you to determine. When the grid is filled, the letters in the outermost ring will spell a bit of sage wisdom from "Red Green" (a.k.a. Steve Smith).

1. *Rock 'n' Roll High School* band, with "the" (−)
2. Makes trippy tees: Hyph. (+)
3. Besmirches (+)
4. Eaves droppers? (−)
5. Part of OCR (+)
6. Assign to an office (+)
7. Oscar-winning actress Young (−)
8. Supposed UFO crash site in New Mexico (−)
9. Considered carefully, as an option (+)
10. Place of suffering in the New Testament (+)
11. Half-conscious states (+)
12. Continue despite stiff opposition (−)
13. First part of Dante's *Divine Comedy* (+)
14. Like some cellphone charges (−)
15. ___ Set (classic toy) (−)
16. *Starring Sally J. Friedman as ___* (Judy Blume book) (−)
17. Expensive watches (−)
18. Gets a move on (+)
19. Little Red Book readers (+)
20. "Court is now in ___" (+)
21. Attacked: 2 wds. (+)
22. Flanders Fields flowers (+)
23. Dwells (−)
24. Reluctance to toot one's own horn (+)
25. Given a sedative before the race, say (+)
26. Girls who prefer treehouses to dollhouses (+)
27. Magicians' props: 2 wds. (−)
28. Director and star of *Modern Times* (+)
29. Make ___ (begin to have an effect) (−)
30. Accept, as terms: 2 wds. (+)
31. Stuff to cook French fries in: 2 wds. (+)
32. Captive whose release is conditional (+)
33. Thom McAn container (−)
34. Skips merrily (+)
35. Marvin ___ (Monopoly property) (−)
36. Rachmaninoff's "___ in C sharp minor" (+)

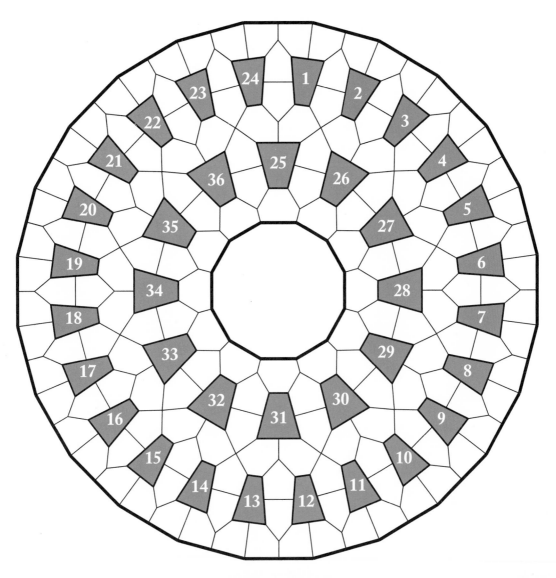

Solution, page 90

Some Assembly Required 3

This 14×14 grid of letters has been chopped into puzzle pieces, and it's up to you to reassemble it. The answer to each numbered clue should be placed in the correspondingly numbered piece, one letter per square, starting in the numbered square. Each row (A–N) in the "tray" contains two answers placed side by side; their clues are given in order, but it's up to you to determine the dividing point between answers. Use the Row answers and the pieces' shapes to determine the proper location of each piece within the tray. You won't need to overlap or rotate any of the pieces. Correctly placed, the 24 pieces will completely fill the tray.

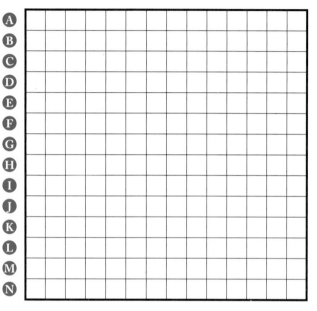

Rows

A Winter Olympics sport since 1964
Puerto Rican actress with a Tony, Oscar, Grammy, and two Emmys: 2 wds.

B The Nile's ___ Dam
Problematic weed in lawns

C Reduce to shreds: 2 wds.
Eczema treatment: 2 wds.

D Like forest sprites
Newswoman whose autobiography was titled *And So It Goes*

E Everyday writers?
Bowstring puller

F Fixes firmly
Purplish fruit used in cobblers

G Maria ___ (Marie Antoinette's mother)
Elements of psychological warfare

H Woolly
Bar man?

I Site of the Parthenon
Make one's beliefs known

J Former astronaut who served on the investigative panels for the *Challenger* and *Columbia* disasters: 2 wds.
What a violin's fingerboard lacks

K Mother-of-pearl source
Patterned socks

L Incurring the EPA's wrath
Gets close to

M Old-fashioned railroad bridge
On the ___ (vigilant): 2 wds.

N Trench warfare excavation: 2 wds.
Packed away

Pieces

1. Quick to recover
2. What Bioré strips are designed to clean
3. Fervor
4. Does some stretches, maybe: 2 wds.
5. 1960s kitchen gadget that sliced and diced: Hyph.
6. Ear-cleaning device: Hyph.
7. Small upright pianos
8. Much-publicized product launch
9. Landlubber's opposite
10. Morally right
11. Where ashes are seen on Ash Wednesday
12. Slow-witted character from the Uncle Remus tales: 2 wds.
13. Mike Wallace's original *60 Minutes* cohost: 2 wds.
14. Bowl or pitcher, e.g.
15. U-shaped geometric curve
16. Unimportant matter
17. What the man of the hour might receive: 2 wds.
18. 1957 musical loosely based on *Romeo and Juliet*: 3 wds.
19. Bygone days
20. Like cash flow in a free market
21. Enjoys oneself immensely: 3 wds.
22. Pierce's successor as Bond
23. Gleaning, as a formula
24. Simile coined by William Tecumseh Sherman: 3 wds.

Solution, page 90

∞ On the Right Track ∞

Words fit into this racetrack-shaped grid in two ways. The Tracks begin just to the right of the shaded "gates" (labeled A to E) and proceed around the grid in figure-eight shapes, ending just to the left of the gates. Clues for each track are given in order, but dividing points between answers are for you to determine. The Lengths are five-letter words or phrases formed on the two outer loops of the track. A numbered space indicates the start of each Length word, with 1 to 12 reading inward and 13 to 23 reading outward.

Tracks

A Gold/silver alloy used to make ancient coins
Works in front of the camera
Beulah of *It's a Wonderful Life*
Prepared grits
Yearbook signers

B Friend, spouse, or family member: 2 wds.
Becoming less reserved
Disagreeable task
On the same elevation as the pin: Hyph.
Method of easing one's labor?

C Oft-repeated words in a historic 1963 speech: 4 wds.
Eroded: 2 wds.
Pleistocene mammal mentioned in a Jean Auel title: 2 wds.
Superstate warring with Oceania in *1984*

D Haute couturier who redesigned the official Boy Scout uniform in 1980: 4 wds.
Add threads to a tapestry
Heavy lifter
Well known in one's field

E Uneasy feeling after a large purchase: 2 wds.
The Biggest ___ (NBC reality show)
Pointless obstructions to progress: 2 wds.
Catches

Lengths

1 *All* ___ *Lead Home* (Peter Boyle's final film)
2 Ready to be operated on
3 Catherine's portrayer in 1939's *Wuthering Heights*
4 Special Forces unit: 2 wds.
5 Single-named 1970s *Hollywood Squares* panelist
6 Whip-cracking circus performer
7 What Tunnel of Love boats might be shaped like
8 "Please," to Planck
9 NBA star known as "The Big Baryshnikov"
10 Mystery novelist Marsh
11 Rolling grassland, in Britain
12 Bedazzled: 2 wds.
13 Messing of *The Starter Wife*
14 With #23, the "nosebleed section" of a stadium
15 *Weekend Edition* host Hansen
16 See eye to eye
17 Polished tabletop's quality
18 City areas rarely mentioned in tourist guidebooks
19 ___ Frist (Anne Heche's *Men in Trees* role)
20 Appliance brand owned by Whirlpool since 2006
21 Weapon infamously used to subdue Andrew Meyer
22 Paperless periodical: Hyph.
23 See #14

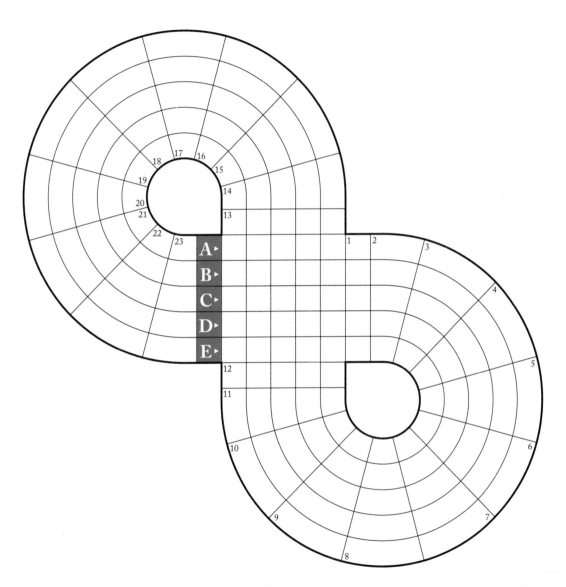

Solution, page 91

Rowed Signs

Each row of a Rowed Signs puzzle contains two consecutive answers placed end to end. Straddling each pair of answers is an "Inner Word"—for example, a row might hold the words DRAGON and YEAR, with the Inner Word AGONY reading between them. Inner Words are clued in random order, so it's up to you to determine which clue goes with which row. As you solve each row, cross out the letters of the Inner Word; when the grid is filled, the remaining letters (reading from left to right by rows) will spell out a sign that might be found at the location specified in the puzzle's heading.

Puzzle 1

Rows

1 Putting in harness, as oxen
   Ballerina's skirt
2 Breath freshener
   At some point: 2 wds.
3 Great destruction
   Require bleeping
4 Small glittery disk
   Mr. White's ace reporter
5 Tree-diagram element
   Film that netted Sir John
      Gielgud an Oscar
6 Attachment: Hyph.
   Things to work on

In the window of the "Subliminal Message Agency"

Inner Words

Recited musically
Severe shortage
Takes place
Breakdown actress Kathleen
"The explanation would only confuse you": 2 wds.
Top 40 hit that premiered on *Saturday Night Live*: 2 wds.

Puzzle 2

Rows

1. More frequented
   Racetrack fence
2. Big name in canned fruit
   Remove pulp from
3. Common element of Victorian architecture
   Haystacks painter
4. Saline drip?
   Collegiate short-timer
5. *The Lost ___ of Jesus* (controversial documentary of 2007)
   Eddie who won horse racing's Triple Crown twice
6. Hallway rug
   ___ Beach, Florida
7. Naturally inclined (to)
   Historic Venetian bridge
8. Takes a turn at the chess table
   Animal serving as Exxon's mascot
9. Look up to
   Put away

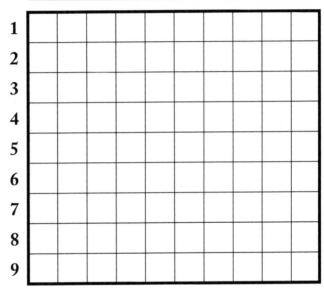

At a Meeting of the "National Procrastination Society"

Inner Words

Into Thin Air setting
Gin-and-tonic garnish
Watering hole on wheels: 2 wds.
Mountain chain
Barely discernable trace
It got FDA approval in 1996
Hall of fame?
Like a defendant: 2 wds.
Disconcert

Snake Charmer 4

Enter the answer to each clue into the grid, starting in the correspondingly numbered space and proceeding clockwise around the S to end in the space before the next consecutive number. The chain of 24 answer words will snake its way around the grid twice.

1 Smart-alecky
2 Enjoyer of large group functions
3 Best player in the NFL at a given position: Hyph.
4 Believer in polytheism
5 Portray unfairly
6 "The thing with feathers / That perches in the soul," according to Dickinson
7 Frequent Scorsese collaborator
8 1986 Keanu Reeves indie about a teenage murderer: 2 wds.
9 Write-your-own-option check box
10 Affliction that ruins a pleasure cruise: 3 wds.
11 Grammy-winning Carole King song of 1972: 3 wds.
12 Problem at overbooked stadiums
13 Clickable words on a Web page
14 Common dog name
15 Like most NBA stars
16 Creator of wartime posters
17 Designed to correct deformity
18 Derived by logic, not observation: 2 wds.
19 Proficient (in)
20 Type of heating used extensively in Iceland
21 Black mark
22 Milkmaid's seat
23 Paid the piper after being proven wrong: 2 wds.
24 Lifeboat

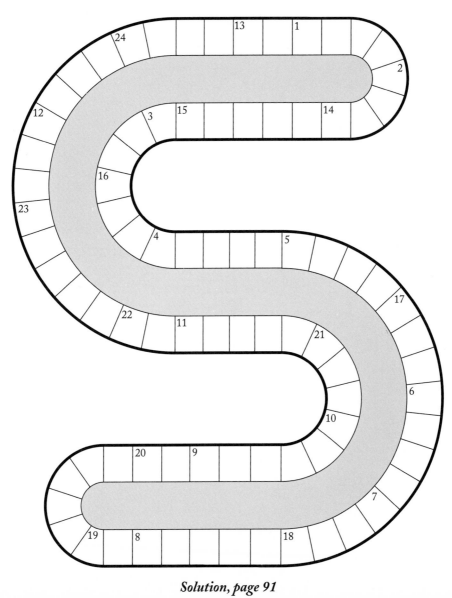

∽ *Horseshoes* ∽

Each numbered stake in the grid is encircled by two "horseshoes"—six-letter words arranged in U-shapes, reading either clockwise or counterclockwise. The sample stake at right, for instance, is encircled by the words ANKLES and KNAVES. The starting points and directions of the answers are for you to determine.

1 Sun's place in the solar system
   Table wine produced in Bordeaux

2 Puts to rest
   Sudden increase in wind speed

3 Temple with stacked roofs
   Salon that offers body treatments: 2 wds.

4 Pileup that blocks progress
   Literary character who hisses "My precious!"

5 Hullabaloo
   Amasses, as a bar tab: 2 wds.

6 Reply
   They're placed in countersunk holes

7 Posted warning
   Frog's fly catcher

8 *The Today Show* movie critic
   There are 3.79 of them in a gallon

9 Sportscaster Ahmad
   Warship fleet

10 Vibraharp striker
   Fred G. Sanford's son

11 Keep ahold of
   Do damage to

12 Assassins in chopsocky films
   Add one's name to the register: 2 wds.

13 2007's Invention of the Year, according to *Time*
   Slovenly "Peanuts" character

14 Mischievous animal in *Caddyshack*
   Writer/director of 2007's *Rescue Dawn*

15 Composer whom Dvorak characterized as "sweet sunshine"
   Phrase that aids in meditation

16 Dumpling served in soup: 2 wds.
   "What do we have to lose?": 2 wds.

17 Cup on a mantelpiece, often
   "The quality of mercy is not strain'd" speaker

18 Original *SNL* cast member Jane
   Diesel fuel burners

19 Vague geographical division
   Delivering an amazing performance, slangily: 2 wds.

20 Swimming spot on *Gilligan's Island*
   Person whose skin lacks melanin

21 Delicacy served by Mexican street vendors
   All grown up

22 Facing
   Treeless plain of the Arctic

23 Conditional release from jail
   Fruit of the *Citrus maxima* tree

24 Keen insight
   Sharp tooth

25 Containing no clumps or clods, say
   Tristan's lover

26 Chess maneuver that sacrifices a piece
   Bar with poles

27 Flasher at a wedding
   Fibbies-dressed-as-sheiks sting operation

28 Sikh's headpiece
   Highwayman

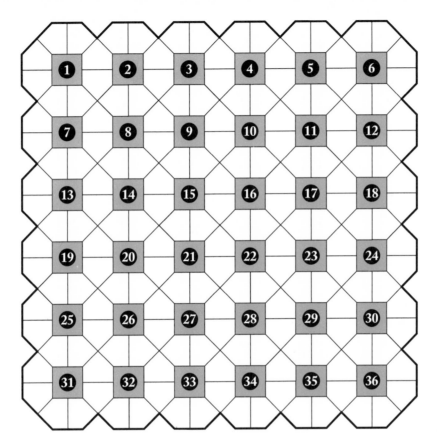

29 Stand around aimlessly
   Toyota model discontinued in 1999
30 Like nature trails
   Places for vases
31 ___ path (equestrian route)
   Clapped eyes on
32 Essential pogo-stick part
   Rolling mill's output

33 One who takes pleasure in being cruel
   Extravagant neckwear
34 Greek odist
   Teddy ___ (animatronic toy)
35 Persian commander at Thermopylae
   Bring to light
36 Whirlpool
   Treasure hunters' finds

Solution, page 91

∞ *Squeeze Play* ∞

This puzzle is like a word search in reverse—you must fit the 44 words and phrases listed below into the grid horizontally, vertically and diagonally, each in a straight line. To fit them all in, though, you'll need to squeeze them—that is, any double-letter combinations in an entry (including those occurring between word breaks, as in HOT TUB) must be squeezed into one of the grid's shaded squares. The word PUZZLE, if entered backward horizontally, would appear as shown. In the completed grid, all of the spaces will be filled.

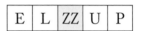

Abbeville	Ellen Terry	inning	root cellar
antenna	fleet of foot	loot	savvy
arraign	fuller	messily	shoo-in
arrive	good deals	middle ear	shrill
attack	Goodall	nugget	stickball
Bill Murray	grass	oddness	tabby cat
Bobby Orr	green apple	Ossian	teethe
butter rum	greets	overruff	too-too
caddy	guess	pep pill	troop
coffin nail	ill will	raccoon	udder
egg roll	illicit	ripple effect	unroof

∽ Rows Garden 4 ∽

Words fit into this flower garden in two ways. Row answers read horizontally from the lettered markers; each Row contains two consecutive answers reading left to right (except Rows A and L, which contain one answer reading across the nine protruding spaces). Blooms are six-letter words or phrases that fill the colored hexagons, reading either clockwise or counterclockwise. Bloom clues are divided into three lists, White, Pink, and Gray; answers from each list should be placed only in the appropriately colored hexagons. All three Bloom lists are in random order, so you must use the Row answers to figure out where to plant each Bloom.

Rows

A Yellow-flowered plant seen hanging around at Christmas

B Genre in which Elvis won all of his Grammys: 2 wds.
Going to work with some company?

C Questions with obvious answers: Hyph.
R.J. Reynolds brand introduced in 1978: 2 wds.

D Street marked by a "No Outlet" sign: Hyph.
Victorian-era pulp magazine: 2 wds.

E Children's game involving a lot of pushing: 4 wds.
Symbolic Valentine's Day gift: 2 wds.

F Country beset for over two decades by "the Troubles": 2 wds.
Cow catcher

G Everyman: 2 wds.
"Incense and ___" (1967 #1 hit)

H Dutch equivalent of Christmas stockings: 2 wds.
Birthplace of Anne of Cleves (no, it's not Cleves)

I Longest undammed river in the contiguous United States
Indisputable but potentially embarrassing facts: 2 wds.

J Get on one's ___ (annoy incessantly)
Malicious, anonymously sent missive: 2 wds., hyph.

K Married women terrified of receiving a telegram: 2 wds.
His "Coconut" appears on the *Reservoir Dogs* soundtrack: 2 wds.

L University where Knute Rockne coached: 2 wds.

White Blooms

Novelty singer Sheb
One of King Arthur's subjects
Dirty Pretty ___ (2002 film)
Christie's female detective
Higher up on the Mohs scale
Grooming aid for "big hair"
Drums played in one's lap
Synthetic fiber used in body armor
Forms foam
Eats, ___ & Leaves (2004 bestseller)
Massachusetts statesman who was infamously caned on the Senate floor
1980 horror film by John Carpenter: 2 wds.
Paperless correspondence: Hyph.
Silver Streak director Arthur

Pink Blooms

Steamboat inventor
Fortunate: 2 wds.
Camp stove fuel

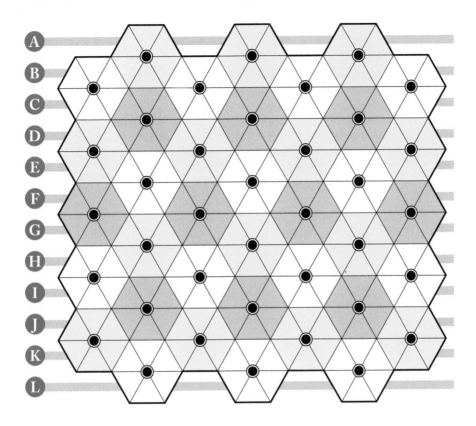

Hieronymus Bosch's *The ___ of Earthly Delights*

Urges on

Guest on Carson's penultimate episode of *The Tonight Show*

Self-assured

Genre played on NPR's *The Thistle & Shamrock*

With a dry wit

Jazz enthusiast

___ Commission (1963 investigative body)

Star of *Venus*

Filtered (through)

Dimmesdale's lover

Gray Blooms

The Muppet Show producer

Contaminates

Pack animals

Balm of ___

Caught some Z's

Mock ___ (*Alice in Wonderland* character)

Annual film-festival site

Answer

Upped the bet, in a game of poker

Romeo and Juliet setting

Solution, page 92

Diamond Rings

Each of this grid's 16 Rings must be filled with two answers reading either clockwise or counterclockwise; both answers will read in the same direction, but their starting points are for you to determine. As an aid to solving, the shaded spaces around the grid's perimeter will "wrap around"—that is, the shaded spaces at the top and bottom will contain the same sequence of letters, and the same goes for the shaded spaces on the sides. The answers to the randomly ordered Diamond clues encircle eight of the grid's nine diamonds; again, their directions and starting points are for you to determine. When the grid is filled, the letters surrounding the unclued diamond will reveal a succinct definition of a diamond ring.

Rings

1 Only actor besides Spencer Tracy to win back-to-back Oscars for Best Actor: 2 wds.
Five-pointed occult symbol

2 Classroom goody-goodies: 2 wds.
Word on a towel

3 Place
Wider purpose: 2 wds.

4 Chevy trucks with car-shaped bodies: 2 wds.
Exerciser's slow, regular running pace: 2 wds.

5 Perceptible to the touch
Team sport played in a pool: 2 wds.

6 Makes shiny, as silverware
Roller coaster's underpinnings

7 Chocolate cake filled with apricot jam: 2 wds.
Male honeybee

8 The "wonderful, wonderful cat" of cartoons
Voice of Princess Fiona in the *Shrek* films: 2 wds.

9 1980s political scandal that implicated Oliver North
American flag worn by a politician, e.g.: 2 wds.

10 Get an audio version of, as an interview: Hyph.
Molotov cocktail container

11 "The Boating Party" painter Mary
Kid's job in an office: 2 wds.

12 Romance novelist Judith
London underwent many of them during the Blitz: 2 wds.

13 Swamp gas, primarily
Conventional adornments

14 Stereotypical inheritors of the earth after a nuclear war
Buy and sell

15 Pass shown to a gate guard: 2 wds.
___ politics (use of government funds for local improvements): Hyph.

16 Porridge-eating trespasser in a folk tale
Willis's young costar in *The Sixth Sense*

Diamonds

Touches up, as old paintings
Quality of a desert
Wooden box in the playroom: 2 wds.
Heed: 2 wds.
Move to a new home
High-ranking clergymen
McIntosh or Rome Beauty, e.g.: 2 wds.
Refreshed the memory of

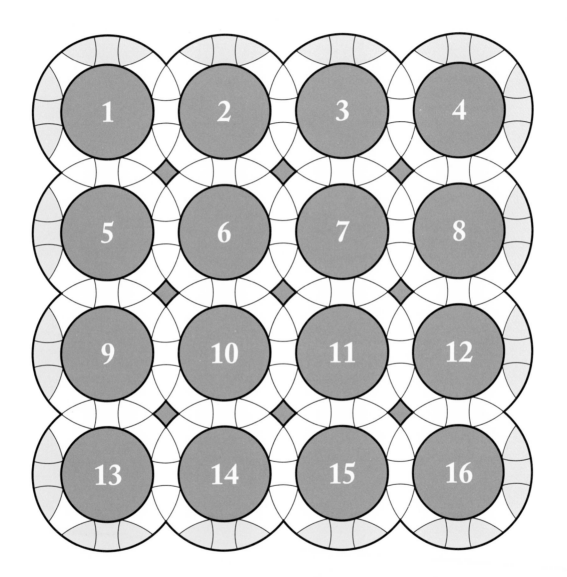

Some Assembly Required 4

This 14×14 grid of letters has been chopped into puzzle pieces, and it's up to you to reassemble it. The answer to each numbered clue should be placed in the correspondingly numbered piece, one letter per square, starting in the numbered square. Each row (A–N) in the "tray" contains two answers placed side by side; their clues are given in order, but it's up to you to determine the dividing point between answers. Use the Row answers and the pieces' shapes to determine the proper location of each piece within the tray. You won't need to overlap or rotate any of the pieces. Correctly placed, the 24 pieces will completely fill the tray.

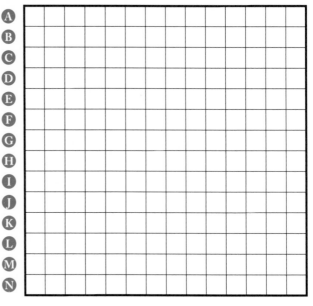

Rows

A Sunday comic strip by Berkeley Breathed
The Pillars of the Earth author: 2 wds.

B Long-winded *Iliad* character
Cheese found in pesto

C Dress down
Conductor's title

D Animated star of the Oscar-winning short *For Scent-imental Reasons*: 3 wds.
Caught with a lasso

E First sign of the zodiac
Adverse comment

F Largest of the Greek islands
Out of practice?

G Oscar Wilde's *An Ideal* ___
Newman who played Connie Conehead

H Carry-on luggage item: 2 wds.
Lay bare

I Pueblo village features
Gardening devices

J Clouseau's portrayer
Another name for the chromatic scale: 2 wds.

K Soccer play that involves touching the ball with one's hands: Hyph.
Dances to 1920s jazz

L Offer a more thorough explanation
Mafioso who appeared on a 1986 *Time* cover

M *Master and Commander* director: 2 wds.
Like some cheddar cheese

N Backrest on a motorcycle: 2 wds.
Archipelago belonging to Portugal

Pieces

1 Stubble remover
2 Students who dress for success, slangily
3 Short amino-acid chains
4 ___ *(The Book)* (2004 bestseller by the writers of *The Daily Show*)
5 Chicago's chief airport
6 Regards: 2 wds.
7 Helped to get through a bad patch: 2 wds.
8 Angered the FCC, perhaps
9 "I can already guess what happened": 3 wds.
10 Devotee of luxury and pleasure
11 Movie preceder in times of yore
12 How a big-time rock band promotes its new album: 2 wds.
13 Florida crustacean whose limbs are harvested for food: 2 wds.
14 Mockery
15 Focus of Michael Moore's *Sicko*
16 Burst forth
17 Foals that are no longer nursing
18 Slow riser
19 Either of two wicked *Cinderella* characters
20 Psychological conflict: 3 wds.
21 Fitness consultants
22 Ill will
23 Backing group for "The Boss," with "the": 3 wds.
24 Cheesy love poem's opening line: 3 wds.

Solution, page 92

❧ *Stained Glass* ❧

Each Inward answer starts in the correspondingly numbered space in the outer ring and continues toward the center of the grid, ending in the space next to the same number. Each Outward answer does the reverse, starting in the inner ring and ending in the outer ring. In the example shows at right, the word TIEPIN reads inward while NITWIT reads outward. It's up to you to determine whether a given word detours around the diamond to the left or right. In each case, the Inward answer will go to one side while the matching Outward answer will go to the other.

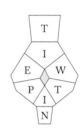

Inward

1 Not as well secured
2 "The Grass Is Blue" singer Dolly
3 In a way: 2 wds.
4 Sportsman who competes on a piste
5 Sergeant or corporal, e.g.
6 Branched horn
7 Became infuriated: 2 wds.
8 Prepare your own gift to be somebody else's gift, say
9 *Balm in* ___ (Lanford Wilson play)
10 Sets aside
11 Falcons' weapons
12 Make back, as losses
13 Broadway musical spelling bee county
14 California's ___ Cucamonga
15 Film that required Kevin Costner to take golf lessons: 2 wds.
16 Once again declare
17 From the Buckeye State
18 Cal Ripken Jr., for one

Outward

1 Alter to fit new needs
2 "Forget it": 2 wds.
3 Pages folded to make booklets
4 Aid for the poor
5 Application made to a judge
6 Part of the eye that contains rods and cones
7 Alluvial plains
8 WWII German tank
9 Gulf of ___ (Baltic Sea inlet)
10 *A Streetcar Named Desire* yell
11 Trail-grooming vehicle at a ski resort: Hyph.
12 One propelling a boat by using a pole
13 Fictional: Hyph.
14 "What a disaster this is!": 2 wds.
15 Opinionated talking head
16 Amazement
17 Largest Native American tribe, today
18 Six Flags Great Adventure roller coaster unveiled in 2006: 2 wds.

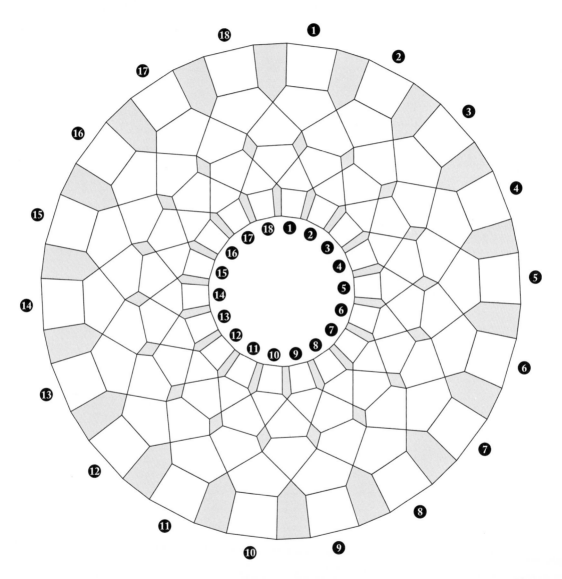

Solution, page 93

Shapeshifters

The two staircase-shaped halves of a Shapeshifter puzzle are designed to be pushed together in two different ways, horizontally and vertically. A horizontal push creates shorter words (or "Shorts"); a vertical push creates longer words ("Longs"). The example below shows a completed Shapeshifter grid and the grids that result from pushing it both ways. The lists of clues given for each puzzle's Shorts and Longs are not in order; it's up to you to determine where the answers go by working back and forth between the two lists.

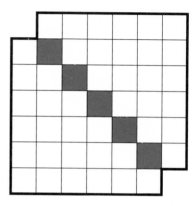

Shorts
Surname of three literary sisters
A time traveler might visit it
Pivotal moment in a novel
Declare to be true
Take big steps
Meditative exercise: 2 wds.
1988 cop drama starring Sean
  Penn

Longs
Haute ___ (high fashion)
Prevailing weather conditions
They might keep tape measures
  around their necks
Showing the most girth
Acne treatment brand
What the trachea divides into

Example

Shorts

Longs

Puzzle 2

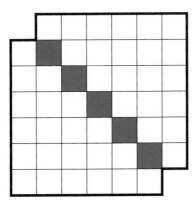

Shorts
Bird known for stealing shiny objects
Perennially ill-tempered person
___ Lachance, narrator of *Stand by Me*
Leader targeted by the Bay of Pigs
   invasion
Author of over 100 western novels
Word before cord or column
Aid a cause, maybe

Longs
What Popeye usually requires before
   beating up Bluto
Offering no second chance, as a
   situation: Hyph.
"Liquid engineering" oil brand
Shelfmate of *Vogue* and *Elle*
Big wheel in the business world
Concert tour hanger-on

Puzzle 3

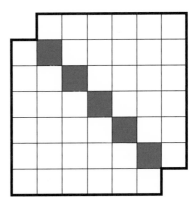

Shorts
Schwarzenegger's costar in *Twins*
Driveway surface that hurts bare
   feet
Go underground
The World Cup, for one
Knitted baby shower gift
In addition: 2 wds.
Insultingly small

Longs
Biographer whose name now means
   "biographer"
What carnitas might be used to fill
Waste away from disuse
Oscar winner for *Shakespeare in
   Love*
Aficionado
How a prognosis might be delivered

Solution, page 93

∽ Snake Charmer 5 ∽

Enter the answer to each clue into the grid, starting in the correspondingly numbered space and proceeding clockwise around the S to end in the space before the next consecutive number. The chain of 25 answer words will snake its way around the grid twice.

1 Likely place to find fossils: 2 wds.
2 *The Forbidden Kingdom* star Jackie
3 Like frat-party antics
4 ___ *Live at the Acropolis* (multi-platinum 1994 album)
5 V-shaped indentation
6 Casey who voiced Shaggy on *Scooby-Doo*
7 Traitorous act
8 Knob on a pipe organ
9 1991 #1 hit for Color Me Badd: 4 wds.
10 One too quick to predict calamity
11 Val Kilmer's *Top Gun* role
12 Hiree who makes a killing?
13 Spaceflight program between Mercury and Apollo
14 GPS tracking system available in GM autos
15 Golf shot designed to roll onto the green after landing short: Hyph.
16 Like Barack Obama's father
17 1939 film promoted with the line "Garbo laughs!"
18 USMC motto, for short: 2 wds.
19 Vision of the future à la *1984* or *Brave New World*
20 Money, slangily: Hyph.
21 Indifferent to questions of ethics
22 Joyful event for weary soldiers
23 Confederate name of Bull Run
24 Scorch
25 Henchmen

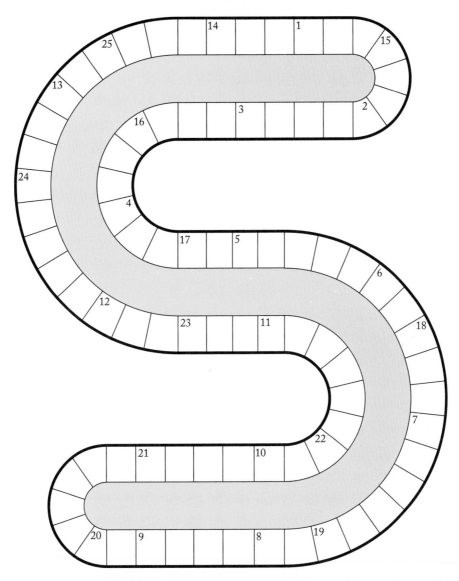

Solution, page 93

⚘ *Forces of Change* ⚘

Each row and column of this grid contains a series of consecutive answers, clued in order of entry. Each row and column also contains one unused square—i.e. a square that the crossing entries are forced to skip over in order to interlock properly. As you find each unused square, fill it with the correct letter to change the corresponding row and column entries into new words. (In one case, the new entry will be a capitalized word.) When the grid is filled, the added letters read from left to right will reveal some forces, while those same letters read from top to bottom will reveal an instrument of change.

Rows

1. Reasons to go to confession
   They're tried again
2. *The Wire* network
   Journey by water
   Horseshoe fastener
   "So that's your game!"
3. Old Dodge model
   Have an effect on
   Bogey beaters
4. Mother of one's cousin
   Ratatouille voice actor Holm
   Mad ___ (party game)
   Closing word of "America the Beautiful"
5. Large deer
   Gas pump unit
   Steel joist: Hyph.
6. Body parts prone to frostbite
   Nautical miles per hour
   Sauce used on white pizza
7. Break-___ (robberies)
   Stead
   Acupuncturist's supply
8. Madrid's Plaza de ___
   Military dining hall
   Emollient-yielding shrub

9. Ellipsis threesome
   Vena ___
   Proportions
10. Oedipus, for one
    Precious stone
    Round in a zookeeper's gun
11. "Haven't you ___?"
    Shallowest of the Great Lakes
    Avoid giving a direct answer
12. Word in two constellation names
    Gave medicine to
    Thin and high-pitched, as a voice
13. Valet
    Start of a famous B-29 bomber's name
    The Decline and Fall of the Roman Empire author
14. Manipulate, as a musical saw
    Dark brown furs
    Ticket counter formation
15. Speedy jets, for short
    Wrecks beyond hope of repair
    Unexpected World Series champs of 1969

Columns

1. Top-Sider, e.g.
   Like games that go into overtime
   All ___ (clumsy)
2. Company known as "Big Blue"
   Actress Maria Conchita ___
   "___ Johnny!"
3. Antiwar demonstrator's sign: 2 wds.
   Lowly member of a kingdom
4. Perform on *American Idol*
   Thin strip of wood
   Consumer choices
5. Command to Fido
   Similar (to)
   The ___ Music in the World (2003 indie film)
6. Hundred Acre Wood creator: 3 wds.
   Stridex user's affliction
   Lennon's "Bed-In" partner
7. *Great Expectations* orphan
   Felipe who managed the Giants
   Glossy periodicals
   Cereal grass

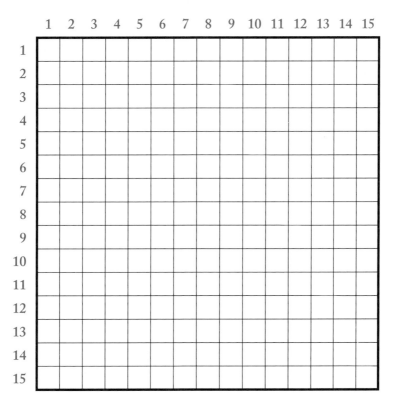

	1	2	3	4	5	6	7	8	9	10	11	12	13	14	15
1															
2															
3															
4															
5															
6															
7															
8															
9															
10															
11															
12															
13															
14															
15															

8 Factory
"I'd sooner die!"
Site of an 1814–15 exile

9 Fences in
Financial support
___ England Club
(Wimbledon venue)

10 Legalese language
For each
Goes from the on-ramp to
the highway

11 Cup's edge
Auction calls
Powerless feeling?

12 "I'm sorry to say"
Martin's *Ed Wood* role
Type of clef

13 Pries (into)
Charles Lamb's nom de
plume
___ card (payment
method)

14 Menacing avowal
___ Mei-ling (Chiang
Kai-shek's wife)
Actor Adams who voiced
Inspector Gadget

15 The Cubs' all-time home run
leader
Tavern frequented by Homer
Simpson
Macroeconomics founder
John Maynard ___

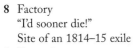

Solution, page 93

∞ *Overlappers* ∞

Each clue in this puzzle leads to a word or phrase that must be entered in the six hexagonal spaces circling the correspondingly numbered hexagon in the grid, reading either clockwise (+) or counterclockwise (−) as indicated. The answers are all at least seven letters long, though, so each answer must overlap itself by one or more letters. For example, HOGWASH, SEAHORSE, and INGESTING are all overlapping words. The starting point of each answer is left for you to determine. As a solving aid, the sides of the grid "wrap around"—that is, the same sequence of letters will read down both of the grid's shaded columns.

1 Like a singing duo's harmonies: Hyph. (−)
2 Small fruit-filled treat (+)
3 Authorize (−)
4 Buy shares of: 2 wds. (+)
5 Square on both sides: Hyph. (+)
6 *The ___ Boy* (Terence Rattigan play) (−)
7 Cost of doing business (−)
8 ___ sports (dangerous activities) (+)
9 Most uncompromising (+)
10 Takes up the cause of (−)
11 Reaches the highest level: 2 wds. (+)
12 Faithful wife of Odysseus (−)
13 Offers relief to (+)
14 Even though: 3 wds. (−)
15 Conniving coward (+)
16 Shawls worn by vaqueros (+)
17 A decongestant might clear them (+)
18 Opened, as a packet: 2 wds. (−)

19 What a gin player must do after drawing (−)
20 Only too aware of one's mistake (+)
21 Traditional tepee material: 2 wds. (−)
22 Fabulously wealthy comic book character: 2 wds. (+)
23 Like unscrupulous moneylenders (−)
24 2007 fantasy film based on a Neil Gaiman novel (+)
25 Hangover symptom (+)
26 Auto race warmup: 2 wds. (−)
27 Very conspicuous, as an error (+)
28 ___ acid (another name for vitamin B_3) (+)
29 Urge on to victory: 2 wds. (−)
30 Hamlet in *Hamlet*, e.g.: 2 wds. (−)
31 Where to buy tees at a golf resort: 2 wds. (+)
32 Rubber used to make O-rings (−)

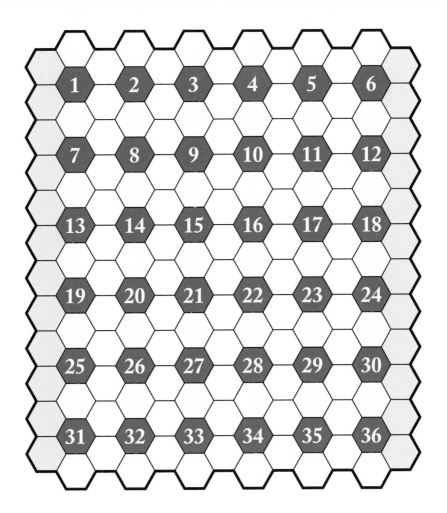

33 Fencer's cry: 2 wds. (+)
34 Landlocked nation bordering Turkey and Iran (−)
35 Carnival where everyone wears Elizabethan garb, for short: 2 wds. (+)
36 Box ___ (fundraising events) (+)

∽ *Rows Garden 5* ∽

Words fit into this flower garden in two ways. Row answers read horizontally from the lettered markers; each Row contains two consecutive answers reading left to right (except Rows A and L, which contain one answer reading across the nine protruding spaces). Blooms are six-letter words or phrases that fill the colored hexagons, reading either clockwise or counterclockwise. Bloom clues are divided into three lists, White, Pink, and Gray; answers from each list should be placed only in the appropriately colored hexagons. All three Bloom lists are in random order, so you must use the Row answers to figure out where to plant each Bloom.

Rows

A Russian composer whose final ballet was *The Tale of the Stone Flower*

B Surpass all others in a bad way: 3 wds.
Spinning broiler used to cook whole chickens

C Having no fixed final date, as an agreement: Hyph.
Recreational facilities for golfers: 2 wds.

D Observed
LAPD-detective-turned-author who wrote *The Onion Field*: 2 wds.

E Annual search conducted by kids: 3 wds.
Glenn Miller's instrument

F It's stuck between teeth: 2 wds.
Research institutes that offer policy advice: 2 wds.

G Estimate that's probably not far off: 2 wds.
1960s musical subgenre typified by Iron Butterfly: 2 wds.

H Bad looking guy?: 2 wds.
Would-be composer's field of study: 2 wds.

I Salt found in fertilizer: 2 wds.
"Getting information off the ___ is like taking a drink from a fire hydrant": Mitchell Kapor

J Shakespearean character whose handkerchief gets stolen
Christmas pageant highlight: 2 wds.

K Co-winner of the 2007 Nobel Peace Prize: 2 wds.
Yarn-producing machines of yore: 2 wds.

L Put a label on

White Blooms

Carrying
___ Biggums (recurring character on Comedy Central's *Chappelle's Show*)
Hides, as a treasure chest
Second mentioned
Wears smooth
The Gay Nineties, for one
Mortal ___ (street-fighting arcade game)
Ballgame division
Neptune's largest moon
Small suit?
Capital on the Kansas River
Engrave
Tidy up
Diverts to a different track

Pink Blooms

Ran for one's health
Vacillate
Forest clearings
Straining devices
Act against

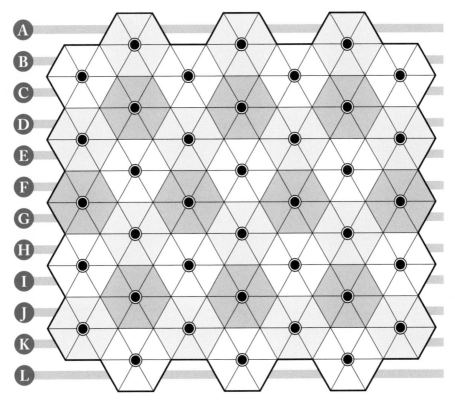

Bush, Clinton, and Bush,
   for example
Pet toy scent, perhaps
2004 Olympic swimming
   champ Ian
Shucking's partner
"Sugar Walls" singer Sheena
Manufacturer of the Red
   Baron's triplane
Big burdens for movers

Displayer of archaeological
   finds
"I just can't stand it any
   longer!"

Gray Blooms
Render bare
Stems used for making
   wickerwork
Sporty two-door cars

Drum set component
Neither small nor large
Worrisome engine noises
___ Creed (early record of
   Christian tenets)
Exchange, as casino chips:
   2 wds.
Played a game at Shinnecock
   Hills
Easy on the eyes

Solution, page 94

The answer to each clue below is entered into the grid as a rectangular "ring" of letters, starting in the numbered space and proceeding clockwise. Each answer begins at one corner of its ring; the symbol before each clue indicates which corner of the ring (so, for example, the answer to clue 1 begins in the upper left corner of its ring). If the answer to #1 were RINGSIDE, it would be arranged in one of the rings shown. The numbers in parentheses after the clues indicate the length of the answer words. If you place all the answers correctly, every space in the grid will be used, and the shaded spaces will contain a well-turned phrase.

^{1}R	I	N
E		G
D	I	S

^{1}R	I
E	N
D	G
I	S

^{1}R	I	N	G
E	D	I	S

1 Kitchen appliance company owned by Electrolux (10)

2 Word popularized by Thomas Kuhn's *The Structure of Scientific Revolutions* (8)

3 Dick Cheney's successor as Secretary of Defense (3,5)

4 Film based on factory worker Crystal Lee Jordan's life (5,3)

5 Grenades, slangily (10)

6 Fictional ship captained by Jonas Grumby (1,1,6)

7 1980s–90s Palestinian uprising against Israeli rule (8)

8 1949 Tracy/Hepburn comedy (5,3)

9 Pop singer Elliot's stage name (4,4)

10 Friend of Harry and Ron at Hogwarts (8)

11 Name in a Tolstoy title (8)

12 In-flight movie's audience (10)

13 Modest (10)

14 President nicknamed "Old Kinderhook" (3,5)

14 1952 biopic based on a Steinbeck book (4,6)

15 Tony-winning star of *Tiny Alice* (5,5)

16 Fixing up (10)

17 Annual betting pool focus (6)

18 Substances used in narcoanalysis (5,5)

19 Show tune that begins "The minute you walked in the joint" (3,7)

20 Martini with a pearl onion garnish (6)

21 Pertaining to money matters (6)

21 Ian Anderson of Jethro Tull, for one (8)

22 Pie with an unusually thick crust (3,5)

23 Appellations such as Prozac and Zyrtec (5,5)

24 Deeply respectful (8)

25 Arrived on the scene (8)

26 Honorific for a Roman Catholic cardinal (4,8)

27 Comic book rival of Betty (8)

28 California State University city (6)

29 Make larger or smaller (6)

30 Tighten one's belt, financially speaking (8)

31 Highly polished flooring (8)

32 Correctly positioned during play (6)

33 Ultimatum issued to indecisive types (3,2,5)

34 1950s filming technique that required three projectors (8)

35 "That's hardly surprising!" (2,6)

1					2		3				
							4		5	6	
	7	8									
				9					10		
11					12					13	
	14						15				
				16		17					18
						19	20				21
22					23	24	25				
	26				27				28	29	
30		31							32	33	
					34		35				

∽ *Section Eight* ∽

The grid below has eight rings and eight sections. Each ring contains a series of words placed end to end, reading either clockwise or counterclockwise; all the words in a given ring read in the same direction. Ring 1 (the outer ring) contains seven answers that read clockwise; the starting spaces are numbered in the grid. Clues for the answers in the remaining rings are given in order, but their starting points and direction are left for you to determine. The sections (separated by the heavy lines radiating from the center) will help you place the inner rings: In a given section, each ring segment contains all but one of the letters in the next segment outward. In other words, a section's outermost segment contains eight letters; the next segment inward contains seven of those eight letters in some order; and so on, until, in Ring 7, only two of the original eight letters remain. No clues are given for the eighth ring; simply choose the right letter from each remaining pair, in order, to spell an appropriate word.

Ring 1
1 Ant lion's "snappers"
2 Activity centers for kids: 2 wds.
3 Brew, as coffee in a glass-topped pot
4 How a wanderer of old might wander: 3 wds.
5 Chessman that moves diagonally
6 Unable to act freely
7 Make more difficult, with "up"

Ring 2
Red blood cell
Scarf made of fur
The Elephant Man insisted he was one, rather than an animal: 2 wds.
"Great Scott!"
Take gas from someone else's tank
Cemetery, in slang
"At least you've got your ___"

Ring 3
Showed off on a surfboard: 2 wds.
Signature tune of Ethel Waters: 3 wds.
Lake ___ Drive (Chicago expressway)
Throb rhythmically
Dolly the Sheep, for one
Aversion that makes bathing difficult
Like office day-care centers: Hyph.

Ring 4
Specification not found in Hoyle: 2 wds.
Metal bowl riddled with holes
Thing worn by a river fisherman: 2 wds.
Prying (into)
Reduced-size versions of pictures

Ring 5
Without a respite
Book that holds loose pages together
Neighborhoods
Radio personality whose regular listeners are known as dittoheads: 2 wds.

Ring 6
By oneself
"Mrs. ___" (1968 #1 single)
Island in the Marianas belonging to the United States
Units divided into pecks

Ring 7
Pungent deli breadstuffs: 2 wds.
Outburst from Ebenezer Scrooge

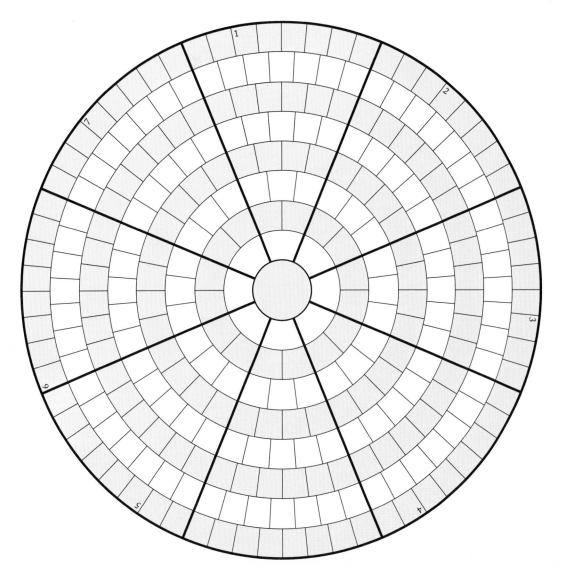

Solution, page 94

∽ *Some Assembly Required 5* ∽

This 14×14 grid of letters has been chopped into puzzle pieces, and it's up to you to reassemble it. The answer to each numbered clue should be placed in the correspondingly numbered piece, one letter per square, starting in the numbered square. Each row (A–N) in the "tray" contains two answers placed side by side; their clues are given in order, but it's up to you to determine the dividing point between answers. Use the Row answers and the pieces' shapes to determine the proper location of each piece within the tray. You won't need to overlap or rotate any of the pieces. Correctly placed, the 24 pieces will completely fill the tray.

Ⓐ Ⓑ Ⓒ Ⓓ Ⓔ Ⓕ Ⓖ Ⓗ Ⓘ Ⓙ Ⓚ Ⓛ Ⓜ Ⓝ

Rows

A Dine out?
Garment worn underneath a sheer bodice

B Up and about
Light that indicates if the power's on: 2 wds.

C South American female
Unchecked development

D Expense
How undervalued workers work: 2 wds.

E Muscle worked by doing push-ups
Cosmetics company for whom Kate Winslet is a spokesmodel

F Ear-piercing
Just barely adequate

G What the sides of a wedge form: 2 wds.
Think (over)

H Extended version
Containing minimal fat

I Attacks the reputation of
Got cozy together on a couch

J Wood that floats
Sends up

K Not too bad to take
Così fan tutte, for one

L Minor disagreement
Competed with in an election: 2 wds.

M Van Gogh's *Café ___ at Night*
Pontiac model introduced in 1973: 2 wds.

N Unusually large TV show casts
Graphic novel from Japan

Pieces

1 *Fargo* sheriff ___ Gunderson
2 Mrs. ___ (word-misusing character in a Sheridan play)
3 Inland waterway
4 Surpass on the shelves

5 Argument that raises eyebrows
6 Hip-hop variety that originated in the Big Apple: 2 wds.
7 Arising from word interpretation, as a dispute
8 Actress who founded the production company Blaspheme Films: 2 wds.
9 *The Rose Tattoo* star Anna
10 Spotlight used by Commissioner Gordon in times of crisis: Hyph.
11 Anthony Hope's *The Prisoner of* __
12 "Love Song" singer Bareilles
13 Direction equivalent to "house right": 2 wds.
14 Head of a school
15 Robbins's role in *The Shawshank Redemption*
16 Folk-music legend Huddie
17 Cream of Wheat competitor: Hyph.
18 High-profile resident of Miami's Federal Correctional Institution since 1992: 2 wds.
19 First woman to sit behind the podium at a State of the Union address: 2 wds.
20 Orbiter designed to photograph Earth from space
21 Last teams standing in the Big Dance: 2 wds.
22 Sentences containing all 26 letters of the alphabet
23 Walks taken for pleasure
24 First book in Cather's *Prairie Trilogy*: 2 wds.

Solution, page 95

∽ *Snake Charmer 6* ∽

Enter the answer to each clue into the grid, starting in the correspondingly numbered space and proceeding clockwise around the S to end in the space before the next consecutive number. The chain of 24 answer words will snake its way around the grid twice.

1 Sash worn over a tunic
2 Head out the door
3 Street musician dressed in a charro outfit
4 Cold appetizers at Luigi's
5 Wood used in barbecue pits
6 Makeshift guest bed
7 Title role portrayer in 2006's *Marie Antoinette*: 2 wds.
8 Harmonious relations
9 Ultra-famous
10 Of ancient Greece
11 Piece keeper?
12 Take a breather
13 NYC theater district
14 Dorothy's surname in *The Wizard of Oz*
15 Schubert composition featured in *Fantasia*: 2 wds.
16 Red table wine from Tuscany
17 Agreeable distractions
18 "You make an excellent point": 2 wds.
19 Mystics who sleep on beds of nails
20 Care for
21 Remove, as a parachute
22 Neoclassical house's covered entrance
23 *Star Trek* actress who stayed on the show at the urging of Martin Luther King Jr.: 2 wds.
24 Opposite of aquatic

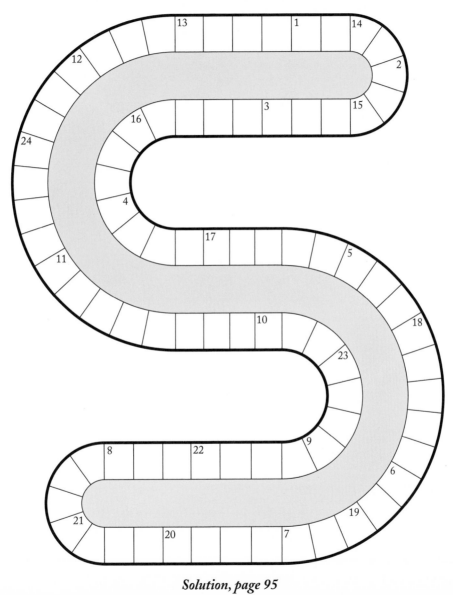

Solution, page 95

81 ⌀

T Squares

Each answer in this puzzle contains at least three letters that form a palindromic sequence—that is, a sequence that reads the same backwards and forwards. Your job is to place the answers into the grid in T-shaped sections, allowing each entry to "double back" on itself. Start each answer in the numbered square and proceed (at least at first) in the direction of the pointer. For example, the word WILDLIFE could appear in the grid in any one of the arrangements shown. You know from the clue number and pointer where the first two letters go; after that, you're on your own.

1 Pertaining to a Jewish house of worship (9)
2 In an asymmetrical fashion (8)
3 Monument on England's Salisbury Plain (10)
4 Paper chaser's ultimate prize (7,6)
5 Number on a "We ID" sign, maybe (5,3)
5 Person whose life has gone astray (4,4)
6 Stop in (5)
7 Strenuous (6)
8 Told secrets to (8,2)
9 Making no sound whatsoever (9)
10 Airhead (5,4)
11 Move in circles (6)
12 Quality of uncomfortable social situations (9)
13 Cool concession-stand treat (3-4)

14 Jane Fonda's costar in *Fun With Dick and Jane* (6,5)
14 ___ Purchase (region bought from Mexico in 1854) (7)
15 1986 comedy featuring Burt Lancaster and Kirk Douglas as paroled gangsters (5,4)
16 You might make a hash of them (8)
16 Kick upstairs (7)
17 WWII prison camp (6)
18 Run-D.M.C.'s paean to a set of sneakers (2,6)
18 Voice that never varies (8)
19 Like biting satire (10)
20 Eldest sister in a 1950s–70s vocal quartet (6,6)
21 Poe short story, with "The" (5,3)
21 Release new software to a limited audience (4-4)
22 Covered wagons crossed them (8)

23 Camelot, for one (6)
24 What vinegar is, essentially (6,4)
25 Tree that doesn't change much with the seasons (9)
26 Some St. Lawrence Seaway segments (6)
27 Flint is a form of it (6)
28 Films that won't be coming to a theater near you (4,6)
28 Inept member of the cast (3,5)
29 Be short with (4,2)
30 How dandies are dressed (2,3,5)
31 All set to go to print (6-5)
32 Bullring performers (7)
33 Popeyed comedian who was a regular on Steve Allen's *Tonight* show (3,6)
34 Beverage originally sold as a patent medicine (4-4)
35 Mythical lizards with fatal gazes (9)

Rows Garden 6

Words fit into this flower garden in two ways. Row answers read horizontally from the lettered markers; each Row contains two consecutive answers reading left to right (except Rows A and L, which contain one answer reading across the nine protruding spaces). Blooms are six-letter words or phrases that fill the colored hexagons, reading either clockwise or counterclockwise. Bloom clues are divided into three lists, White, Pink, and Gray; answers from each list should be placed only in the appropriately colored hexagons. All three Bloom lists are in random order, so you must use the Row answers to figure out where to plant each Bloom.

Rows

A Aerates the soil in a vegetable garden

B A ball is periodically dropped here: 2 wds.
Final #1 hit from Michael Jackson's *Bad* album: 2 wds.

C Be overly pushy: 3 wds.
Worsted fabric used for suits

D Sautéed delicacies served at Red Lobster: 2 wds.
Depicted on one's escutcheon

E Silent horror film featuring the villainous Count Orlok
Performed sit spins and pigeonwings: Hyph.

F 1982 blockbuster taglined "It knows what scares you"
Like beer in unlabeled bottles, perhaps: Hyph.

G Auto exec who oversaw the design of the Lincoln Continental: 2 wds.
1980s Ricky Schroder sitcom: 2 wds.

H Scouring pad brand: Hyph.
SNL performer who invented the Bass-O-Matic: 2 wds.

I Military decorations that indicate the length of a soldier's tenure: 2 wds.
Lays out flat, as a carpet

J Real-life examples used by social scientists: 2 wds.
Where a color war might be fought: 2 wds.

K Some Christmas decorations
Medals engraved with the profile of George Washington: 2 wds.

L Like donkeys and jackrabbits: Hyph.

White Blooms

Rouse to action
What frivolous romantic partners can't do
Food poisoning symptom
Exchanges blows
Get ready: 2 wds.
Animal used to drive rabbits from their burrows
Luke's father in the *Star Wars* saga
Music written for movies
Famous British insurance market, for short
Country singer Yearwood
Lackadaisical workers take lots of them
Showy goal shot in soccer
Danson's role on *Cheers*
There are eight in a peck

Pink Blooms

Like most phone numbers
Span of many a DVD box set
Person you might see a lot of?
Mall's many

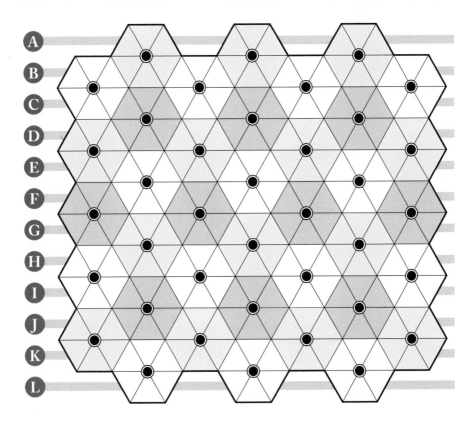

1985 comedy featuring Chevy Chase in a variety of disguises
Pastoral poetry
Thoroughgoing: Hyph.
Hoboes
Battle between street gangs
Iconic teen sex comedy of 1982

Whale on with one's fists
Paper cutter?
Major part of a squirrel's diet
Damaged in a hailstorm, say

Gray Blooms
Gothic architecture features
Birchbark boats

Mountains of Missouri
Boots out
Howe known as "Mr. Hockey"
Loofah
Set at an angle
Take away
Where a boxer sits between rounds
Really impressed, slangily

Solution, page 95

85 ∞

Sundial

Some Assembly Required 1

A	F	O	R	M	S	S	A	M	E	T	O	Y	O	U
B	L	O	D	E	S	T	O	N	E	P	E	R	C	H
C	E	V	A	D	E	D	E	T	C	E	T	E	R	A
D	S	E	R	I	E	S	E	P	I	P	H	A	N	Y
E	D	R	Y	A	S	A	B	O	N	E	S	T	A	R
F	E	N	G	O	R	G	E	H	Y	G	I	E	N	E
G	G	I	L	L	I	A	N	G	A	O	L	E	R	S
H	H	E	A	D	P	I	N	S	T	N	O	T	E	S
I	T	R	I	E	S	O	N	P	H	I	N	E	A	S
J	C	U	B	A	N	I	D	I	O	C	R	A	C	Y
K	D	R	U	P	E	D	E	E	P	S	I	X	E	S
L	E	C	O	M	M	E	R	C	E	T	W	I	S	T
M	P	R	E	T	E	N	S	E	D	E	A	F	E	R
N	P	A	C	M	A	N	S	E	L	E	C	T	E	E

Projectors

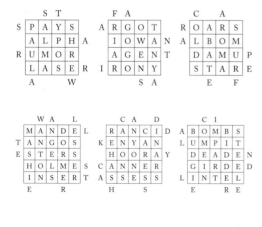

```
        S T              F A              C A
   S  P A Y S       A  R G O T       R  O A R S
   A  L P H A       I  I O W A N     A  L B O M
   R  U M O R       A  A G E N T     D  D A M U P
   L  L A S E R     I  I R O N Y     S  S T A R E
        A   W            S A              E   F

        W A L            C A D            C I
   M A N D E L     R A N C I D       A B O M B S
   T A N G O S     K E N Y A N       L U M P I T
   E S T E R S     H O O R A Y       D E A D E N
   H O L M E S     C A N N E R       G I R D E D
   I N S E R T     A S S E S S       L I N T E L
        E   R            H   S            E   R E
```

Rows Garden 1

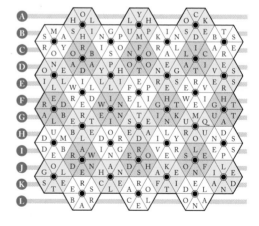

Boxing Rings 1

```
C H E N T E E L A R I M B
S E M X A I S F S E N S U
T S I N L A C I T P G R A
B U G E R R E X C A T E D
Y B S S J U L I O N S P E
D A L I Z D L T C U R I F
N R A M E G O P E S I N T
A C T I V E T O S I O O M
N O I T A H C R A B N T E
O M C I D A A S R B A T N
R E D N N N E R P I O N P
T R Y T A N D A E T S E E
S A P S B A C S T P E C R
```

Snake Charmer 1

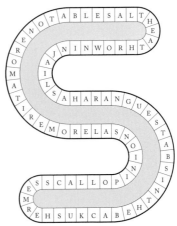

Cloud Nine

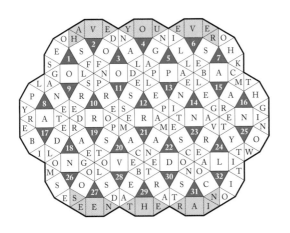

Game Hunting

```
B A L K S L I P S R A N G U P
A M I N O I D A H O N O R S E
D I N E T T E T A W D R I E R
E D G E H E A R H E R A L D S
G R O W E R A I S L E E L M O
G O F E R S S A M B A T H A N
B U L L E T T R A Y S H A R P
L E E D S R A C Y E M I L I O
I N A S M U C H A S I C O N S
S P E C I A L R B I A S S E T
S A M E R N I E E N T H U S E
I M P A C T E D A K A A N N A
S E T S H U N S R E O R D E R
A L O E E M T E U R O P E A N
Y A R D S A S A P S H O R T S
```

Some Assembly Required 2

A	H	E	S	S	C	I	N	D	E	R	E	L	L	A
B	C	A	S	S	E	T	T	E	S	R	E	L	I	C
C	S	Q	U	A	L	L	I	N	G	N	A	I	V	E
D	D	E	A	T	H	C	A	B	L	E	C	A	R	S
E	E	E	R	I	E	P	I	L	E	D	I	T	O	N
F	P	R	I	O	R	P	E	T	E	R	N	E	R	O
G	A	S	U	N	D	E	R	H	A	T	S	O	F	F
H	T	O	M	E	S	O	P	T	I	N	G	F	O	R
I	N	T	H	D	E	G	R	E	E	G	U	L	L	S
J	A	P	R	O	P	O	S	T	U	X	E	D	O	S
K	S	A	L	M	A	G	I	N	G	E	R	A	L	E
L	I	M	M	U	N	I	T	I	E	S	B	O	D	Y
M	P	O	T	R	O	A	S	T	S	T	R	A	P	S
N	S	W	O	R	N	E	N	E	M	Y	S	U	E	S

Snake Charmer 2

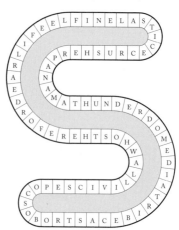

Riding the Waves

Rows Garden 2

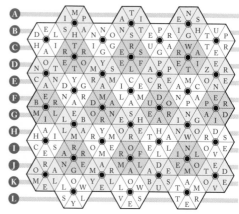

Block Lettering

A PRIL	P LAID	L OPEZ	Z ELIG	E LIZA
R ODAN	D ROPS	O GLED	G IZMO	I MAGE
N ORSE	S EDAN	E PSOM	M ARGE	A XIOM
O CEAN	A ESOP	P EARL	R OMPS	O PRAH
C ODEX	E CLAT	L APSE	S LURP	P IOUS
X ACTO	T EXAS	A DULT	U SAIR	I NPUT
A XLES	S TAND	D RAWS	R OUND	N ICER
E VIAN	N EWSY	W OUND	O WNER	E BONY

Twist Ties

Snake Charmer 3

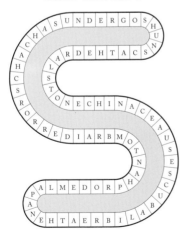

Boxing Rings 2

S	H	E	R	E	M	M	A	R	E	D	S	D
W	A	C	Y	N	O	A	L	E	D	N	U	E
O	R	C	L	E	T	J	R	C	H	E	D	A
L	E	B	E	A	R	O	E	T	E	S	M	C
P	S	T	T	S	M	O	K	I	T	S	E	C
X	E	E	K	R	A	S	C	N	O	N	N	R
S	M	R	E	E	R	R	A	J	N	I	T	E
B	I	B	H	I	M	A	L	O	R	E	M	S
U	N	G	R	Z	A	R	F	E	C	N	A	J
S	I	M	E	Z	C	E	T	R	A	S	S	A
D	T	E	N	O	R	L	C	A	L	R	T	K
R	A	V	O	M	A	L	E	P	S	E	A	P
E	N	I	M	A	L	U	K	S	S	T	R	O

Packing Slips

T	H	E	N	C	E	V	E	R	O	B	E	A	C	H
G	A	I	N	O	N	S	O	R	T	S	T	I	L	L
R	O	M	A	N	I	A	P	R	O	U	D	E	S	T
F	A	N	T	A	P	O	T	S	L	E	G	E	N	D
L	O	S	E	R	S	H	E	E	P	L	O	O	N	S
B	L	A	M	E	M	O	S	E	S	S	C	A	N	T
Z	E	R	O	R	A	I	S	I	N	S	W	I	N	E
S	T	U	B	L	E	T	S	E	A	T	M	A	L	L
A	N	G	E	L	A	T	I	T	L	E	D	E	E	D
C	H	I	N	O	U	S	H	E	R	S	C	H	W	A
E	S	T	H	E	R	N	E	A	T	O	L	A	R	D
C	O	N	G	E	S	T	T	I	E	R	L	Y	L	E
R	A	T	S	H	E	M	M	E	D	R	E	B	A	R
I	N	G	O	I	N	G	L	I	D	S	C	O	R	D
M	A	R	X	W	A	Y	N	E	O	T	T	E	R	S

Rows Garden 3

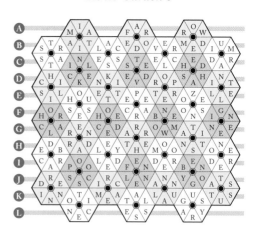

Seven Sages

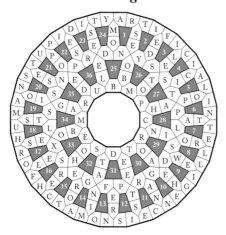

Some Assembly Required 3

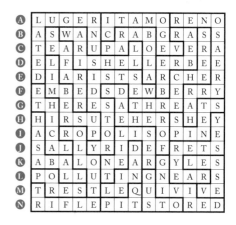

A	L	U	G	E	R	I	T	A	M	O	R	E	N	O
B	A	S	W	A	N	C	R	A	B	G	R	A	S	S
C	T	E	A	R	U	P	A	L	O	E	V	E	R	A
D	E	L	F	I	S	H	E	L	L	E	R	B	E	E
E	D	I	A	R	I	S	T	S	A	R	C	H	E	R
F	E	M	B	E	D	S	D	E	W	B	E	R	R	Y
G	T	H	E	R	E	S	A	T	H	R	E	A	T	S
H	H	I	R	S	U	T	E	H	E	R	S	H	E	Y
I	A	C	R	O	P	O	L	I	S	O	P	I	N	E
J	S	A	L	L	Y	R	I	D	E	F	R	E	T	S
K	A	B	A	L	O	N	E	A	R	G	Y	L	E	S
L	P	O	L	L	U	T	I	N	G	N	E	A	R	S
M	T	R	E	S	T	L	E	Q	U	I	V	I	V	E
N	R	I	F	L	E	P	I	T	S	T	O	R	E	D

On the Right Track

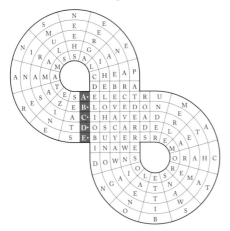

Rowed Signs

Snake Charmer 4

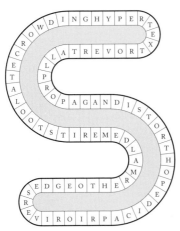

Horseshoes

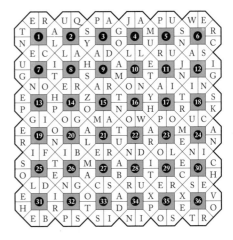

Squeeze Play

S	A	VV	Y	A	RR	U	M	LL	I	B	N
T	SS	DD	TT	O	DD	N	E	SS	E	U	G
I	A	A	Y	E	T	R	R	V	GG	TT	I
C	C	BB	R	A	CC	OO	N	E	I	E	A
K	O	E	Y	G	T	F	T	G	LL	RR	RR
B	FF	V	N	C	R	L	OO	OO	W	U	A
A	I	I	E	R	A	EE	L	DD	I	M	F
LL	NN	LL	Y	RR	E	T	N	E	LL	E	LL
I	A	E	I	H	U	O	N	A	I	SS	O
R	I	D	T	C	E	FF	EE	L	PP	I	R
H	L	EE	OO	N	I	OO	H	S	E	L	GG
S	T	EE	R	G	A	T	R	OO	P	Y	E

Rows Garden 4

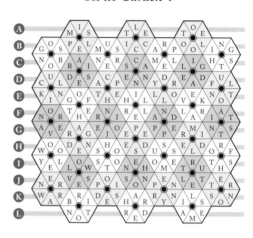

Diamond Rings

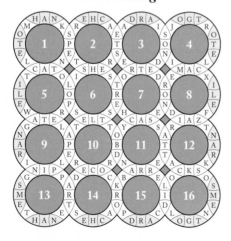

Some Assembly Required 4

O	P	U	S	K	E	N	F	O	L	L	E	T	T
N	E	S	T	O	R	P	A	R	M	E	S	A	N
R	E	P	R	O	V	E	M	A	E	S	T	R	O
P	E	P	E	L	E	P	E	W	R	O	P	E	D
A	R	I	E	S	S	T	R	I	C	T	U	R	E
C	R	E	T	E	D	I	S	B	A	R	R	E	D
H	U	S	B	A	N	D	L	A	R	A	I	N	E
T	O	T	E	B	A	G	U	N	C	O	V	E	R
L	A	D	D	E	R	S	W	E	E	D	E	R	S
S	E	L	L	E	R	S	T	O	N	E	R	O	W
T	H	R	O	W	I	N	L	I	N	D	I	E	S
E	L	U	C	I	D	A	T	E	G	O	T	T	I
P	E	T	E	R	W	E	I	R	S	H	A	R	P
S	I	S	S	Y	B	A	R	A	Z	O	R	E	S

Stained Glass

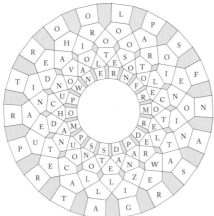

Shapeshifters

Snake Charmer 5

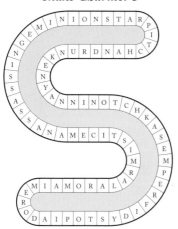

Forces of Change

The added letters spell VOLUNTEER ARMIES left to right, and UNIVERSAL REMOTE top to bottom.

Overlappers

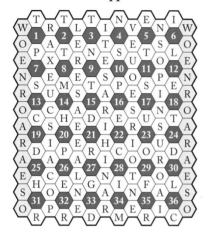

Rows Garden 5

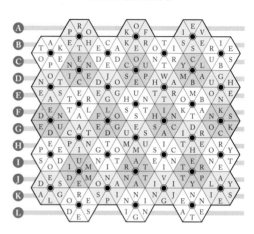

Boxing Rings 3

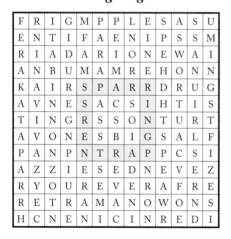

Section Eight

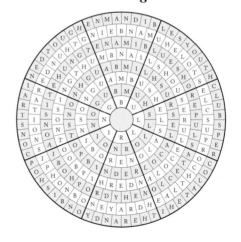

Some Assembly Required 5

A	P	I	C	N	I	C	C	A	M	I	S	O	L	E
B	A	S	T	I	R	P	I	L	O	T	L	A	M	P
C	L	A	T	I	N	A	R	A	M	P	A	N	C	Y
D	C	O	S	T	F	O	R	P	E	A	N	U	T	S
E	T	R	I	C	E	P	S	L	A	N	C	O	M	E
F	S	H	R	I	L	L	M	A	R	G	I	N	A	L
G	A	C	U	T	E	A	N	G	L	E	M	U	L	L
H	E	L	O	N	G	A	T	I	O	N	L	E	A	N
I	D	E	F	A	M	E	S	S	P	O	O	N	E	D
J	B	A	L	S	A	S	A	T	I	R	I	Z	E	S
K	E	N	D	U	R	A	B	L	E	O	P	E	R	A
L	T	I	F	F	R	A	N	A	G	A	I	N	S	T
M	T	E	R	R	A	C	E	G	R	A	N	D	A	M
N	E	N	S	E	M	B	L	E	S	M	A	N	G	A

Snake Charmer 6

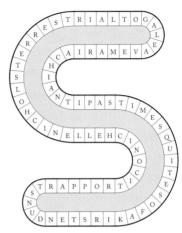

T-Squares

T	S	O	U	L	A	G	E	S	A	C	E
C	Y	L	N	E	V	R	I	T	P	A	T
O	N	E	C	S	I	O	N	O	S	M	O
L	A	G	O	S	T	E	G	N	E	H	R
L	T	E	N	S	H	G	U	O	T	A	P
E	S	Y	F	E	S	A	Y	M	A	T	O
G	E	D	I	N	E	D	S	N	B	E	E
R	I	A	R	P	H	I	P	A	L	S	S
E	V	E	R	A	T	A	K	C	A	T	K
E	O	M	E	N	O	N	N	E	L	I	S
N	H	A	N	S	T	T	O	T	O	C	A
M	A	C	T	O	R	E	D	I	C	A	B

Rows Garden 6

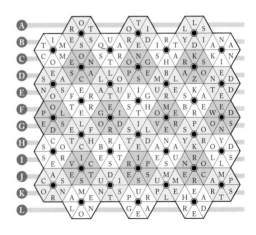

Patrick Berry is a freelance puzzle constructor living in Athens, Georgia. His puzzles have appeared in *The New York Times*, *The Wall Street Journal*, *Harper's*, *The New Yorker*, and numerous other publications. He is also the editor of *The Chronicle of Higher Education*'s weekly crossword.